The Study and Analysis
of
Black Politics

A Bibliography

by

HANES WALTON, JR.

The Scarecrow Press, Inc.
Metuchen, N. J.   1973

Library of Congress Cataloging in Publication Data

Walton, Hanes, 1941-
    The study and analysis of Black politics.

    1. Negroes--Politics and suffrage--Bibliography.
I. Title.
Z1361.N39W29   016.32   73-12985
ISBN 0-8108-0665-7

To Miss Luella Hawkins:

A Very Gifted and Charming Librarian
Who Has Made Many Significant Contributions
to the Study of the Black Past.

Savannah State College Shall Never Be the Same
Since She Has Passed this Way.... For She Has
Enriched the Lives of Many, Both Inside
and Outside the School's Library.

FOREWORD

Which road is the road to freedom? In all ages,
and in countries around the globe, men have stood at the
crossroads and asked themselves this question. And in
mid-twentieth century America, black Americans, like other
oppressed groups that have preceded them, increasingly have
selected politics as at least one of the most important roads
to freedom. Their conviction that concerted political action
could be a mighty force for achieving important freedoms
was strengthened by the great lengths to which the white
South had gone to preclude their exercise of the political
franchise. Thus, blacks in twentieth century America have
had to struggle, first, to achieve the unrestricted right to
use the ballot to advance their cause, and secondly, to use
the ballot in a manner best calculated to gain the essential
ingredients of what most Americans have come to identify
with "the good life." Black political scientists have contributed, and are still contributing to the success of this
second struggle in several significant respects. In the first
place, their studies are "turning on" young blacks to the
potential for constructive change that lies in intelligent
participation in politics. And secondly, by illuminating and
analyzing the successful and the unsuccessful strategies and
tactics employed by blacks in past political struggles, the
studies by black political scientists help point the way to
those strategies and tactics which hold the greatest promise
for the success of present and future efforts.

If politics is indeed a significant road to freedom for black Americans, then black political scientists are helping to build that road. What they are building, however, is superstructure. The sub-structure, the basic foundation, lies in works such as the present one, Hanes Walton's The Study and Analysis of Black Politics: A Bibliography. By providing researchers with comprehensive lists of the essential sources of information in their field, bibliographies greatly facilitate their work, relieving the researcher of the necessity for much of the trial and error following-up of leads which has, of necessity, characterized the efforts particularly of those who have attempted to uncover, correct, and publish the record of black Americans' political strivings. The work by Professor Walton, however, represents sub-structure to a greater extent than most bibliographies. Its topical organization, together with the lucidly written introductory essays for each topic, establishes a framework for research in black politics which should prove helpful to the experienced researcher, and a positive godsend to the novice. Thus it should encourage and stimulate more studies by undergraduate and graduate students, as well as by busy professors, than would otherwise be the case.

Clifton R. Wharton, Jr., in "Reflections on Black Intellectual Power," in the Fall, 1972 issue of the Educational Record, calls for greater effort to be devoted to the building of black intellectual power. Hanes Walton, with his Bibliography, does considerably more than call for the building of intellectual power. He provides in his efforts a model of black intellectual power at work; he supplies some basic tools and resources for bringing black intellectual power to bear on the political process; and in so

vi

doing, he contributes significantly to the sub-structure of not one, but two, important roads to freedom: political power and intellectual power.

Thomas H. Byers
Dean of Faculty
Savannah State College

CONTENTS

PREFACE

This volume represents the first systematic effort
to look at and put in perspective the literature on the political activities of Black Americans. To be sure, there
exist general bibliographies on Blacks in America. Elizabeth E. Miller's The Negro in America[1] is a serious attempt at an extensive, exhaustive and "overdue contribution
to the understanding of America's race relations." There
is also a popular but brief treatment by Erwin K. Welsch,
The Negro In the United States: A Research Guide (Bloom-
ington: Indiana University Press, 1965).

Two bibliographies aimed at different audiences have
also been issued. Erwin A. Salk's A Layman's Guide to
Negro History (New York: McGraw-Hill, 1967) was aimed
at the general public and therefore tended to be simplified
and brief, but it is useful. On the other hand, William L.
Katz prepared an annotated work for school teachers, A
Teacher's Guide to American Negro History (New York:
Quadrangle), which was well received and quite useful.

However, Monroe N. Work's Bibliography of the
Negro in Africa and America (New York: Octagon, 1965)
remains the most indispensable compilation of references to
Blacks before 1928. In addition to Work, Katz, Welsch,
Salk, and Miller, there are numerous other bibliographies,
compiled by groups, centers, institutes, libraries, etc.,
but these are generally hard to locate or are not readily
available in terms of circulations.[2] None of these reference

volumes, in any case, is devoted specifically to Black politics. Some of the books, like those already mentioned, devote a chapter or a sub-chapter to "Politics and Suffrage" but they are far from comprehensive, systematic or analytical. And with the recent reemergence of Blacks into the political mainstream the need for concrete data, for knowledge of trends, patterns and the relationship of earlier political efforts to those of the present, is of immeasurable importance. In short, a guide to Black politics in America is needed for the scholar, the political scientist or the layman. It is equally necessary for the journalist, the reporter or the Black political candidate who is in search of a tradition, a means of strategy and knowledge of past efforts, both successes and failures. The present Black political candidates need to be aware of old platforms, past legislative efforts and continuing needs within the Black community.

The work can also enhance the knowledge of present policy makers and decision makers, as well as those foundations and philanthropists who want to contribute to and assist current Black political efforts toward improvement.

In this vein, then, the present volume was born. First, it tries to assemble all of the significant literature together in one volume. Secondly, it tries to order the literature into categories and topics of concern. Thirdly, it tries to indicate the trends and patterns of the literature and indicate briefly the needs for the future. And lastly, it seeks to introduce the reader to controversial areas and subjects which need serious study and reflection.

In preparing this volume many debts were incurred. Yet there are some individuals whom I must acknowledge in an individual rather than a collective manner, because their contributions went beyond what one could reasonably expect. Miss Luella Hawkins, to whom the volume is dedicated, was more than helpful. She was a guide in a weary land, a knowledgeable traveler who gave unselfishly of her time, advice and kindness. She made a great contribution to the work.

Miss Lillie Mae Key, a graduate student and personal secretary of the first order, nearly wrote the book. She checked and rechecked sources, ran down fugitive articles and made sense of a massive hodge-podge of material. The book could not have been finished without her efforts, which will always be truly appreciated.

Others who were of immense help were: Mrs. Shirley Williams Brown, Mrs. Allen, Miss Sandy Huiett, Mr. Andrew McLemore, Doctor E. J. Dean, Dean Thomas Byers, President Prince A. Jackson, Jr., Professors Delany Sanford, Isaiah McIver, Samuel Dubois Cook, Leslie McLemore, C. Vernon Gray, Alex Willingham and Mack Jones. Thanks are also due to Professor Lenneal Henderson, who was gracious enough to permit me to view an annotated bibliography which he compiled, and which now appears in his book, Black Political Life in America. [3] I am also grateful to Professor Robert Holmes, who took time out of his busy schedule to write an introduction, and to Dean Thomas H. Byers, who did the foreword.

Some readers may notice certain omissions from this bibliography. These omissions may be due to negligence, oversight or intention on my part, but they also grew out of limited facilities at a small Black College. It is hoped, in the final analysis, that the merits outweigh the book's limitations.

Hanes Walton, Jr.
November   1972

Notes

1. Cambridge: Harvard University Press, 1970.

2. For a list of many of these other bibliographies, see Ibid., p. 297-310.

3. A very brief and poorly organized bibliography on Black Politics was done by Professor Gardner. It was only twelve typewritten pages. See Henry L. Gardner, Readings in Contemporary Black Politics (Illinois: Public Affairs Research Bureau of Southern Illinois University, 1969). See also a new and recent Bibliography: Milton D. Morris, The Politics of Black America: An Annotated Bibliography [Illinois: Public Affairs Research Bureau of Southern Illinois University, 1971]. This work concentrates primarily on contemporary publication and is limited to only a few topics.

INTRODUCTION

Twenty years ago it was perhaps possible to read all
the books and articles published on Black politics. However,
during the last decade the literature has expanded so quickly
that it is almost impossible to remain abreast of it. The
growing interest in and research on the Black political experience in America has been reflected in a surfeit of publications on Black politics. Authors with diverse back-
grounds from many disciplines, including professors,
journalists, politicians, political scientists and historians,
sociologists and psychologists, blacks and whites, males
and females, Jews and Gentiles, have contributed works on
the Black political experience in the United States. Keeping
up with this rapidly growing subfield of political science
has indeed become a major problem. Although the literature
is abundant and continues to increase at a very rapid rate,
few systematic efforts have been made to provide a detailed
bibliography of these writings. Among the best bibliographic
studies undertaken on the subject are the very general work
of Elizabeth W. Miller,[1] the more limited study of Lenneal
J. Henderson, Jr.,[2] and the more specialized bibliography
by Hanes Walton, Jr.[3] However, none of these studies
represents an effort to provide a complete listing of research and writings on the many dimensions of Black political
life. This volume differs in that it is more comprehensive
and includes references on the full range of Black politics.

The <u>Study and Analysis of Black Politics: a</u>

Bibliography is an important basic resource work on Black politics, of great value to scholars, journalists, students and others concerned with Black political life in the United States.   In this volume Professor Hanes Walton, Jr. attempts systematically and comprehensively to identify the literature of the past eighty years which deals with the Black political experience.   It contains more than 1,000 references from several disciplines.   The author draws from the literature of sociology, religion, journalism, psychology and history, as well as political science, in presenting the most thorough bibliography that has ever been published on Black politics.

Special attention is given to the areas of blacks and political parties, black pressure groups, black political candidates, black political behavior, and black political thought.   And references are included that relate to other important aspects of Black politics such as the agents of Black political socialization (schools and churches), blacks and public policies, Black political activities at the local, state and national levels, and blacks in the urban and international environment.   Listings contained in the volume include articles from scholarly and popular journals, new books as well as reissues of out-of-print works, pamphlets, newspapers, papers presented at meetings of professional associations, and unpublished masters' theses and doctoral dissertations.   Among the essays included in the study are many from such obscure journals (many have ceased publication) as Arena, Alexander's Magazine, Missionary Review of the World, Opportunity, Outlook, and Sepia Socialite; articles in well known popular magazines and periodicals like Black Politician, Crisis, Ebony, Freedomways, Journal of Negro History, Nation, Negro Digest, and New Republic;

and writings appearing in the official publishing organs of numerous professional associations and other scholarly publications including Annals of the American Academy of Political and Social Science, American Journal of Sociology, Journal of Politics, Phylon, and Political Science Quarterly. The contributions of pioneer researchers, scholars and writers like Ralph Bunche, Clarence Bacote, Robert Gill, Harold Gosnell, Henry Lee Moon and many others who helped make the study of Black politics a lively, engrossing and respectable field of inquiry are listed in the volume.

All those who have engaged in serious research on Black politics will appreciate the enormous amount of labor required to put together a bibliography of this sort. The proliferation of writings on Black politics, particularly since the last decade, are scattered throughout numerous disciplines and various publications. This volume should be a significant tool and resource for teachers and researchers in politics, sociology, education and history, as well as for politicians and bureaucrats concerned with the past, present and future of black politics in America.

Robert A. Holmes
Department of Political Science
Atlanta University

Notes

1. The Negro in America: A Bibliography (New York: Cambridge University Press, 1970).

2. "Black Political Life in the United States: A Bibliographic Essay," in Lenneal J. Henderson, Jr. (ed.), Black Political Life in the United States: A First as the Pendulum (San Francisco: Chandler Publishing Company, 1972), 253-269.

3. "A Bibliography on Black Politics," in Hanes Walton,

Jr., Black Politics: A Theoretical and Structural Analysis (Philadelphia: J. B. Lippincott Company, 1972), 225-239.

Chapter I

BLACK POLITICS: AN OLD AND NEW FIELD

Introduction

Political Science as an intellectual field of endeavor
has a relatively old history.[1] Although it is one of the new
areas of social science, its roots extend far back into the
nineteenth century. And today, with the role of government
and political affairs so pervasive in our society, the study
of politics has gained the interest of many scholars and
laymen.

On the college and the university level the field
began to emerge with a separate status at the very beginning of the twentieth century. By 1904 a professional
association was created. As the complexity of twentieth
century government grew, so did the field and its numerous
sub-fields and areas of specialization.

The trend toward greater specialization in political
science mushroomed after World War II. The field became
so broad and complex that the political scientist, in order
to know more, became limited to less and less. However,
the problem of epistemology in political science, and for
the political scientist, is not our concern here. It touches
upon our interest but is not of major importance in the
context of this bibliography.

It is important to distinguish sub-fields of political
science such as political theory and philosophy, public

1

administration, international relations, comparative politics, political parties, the political process, etc., from area specialization, for example, the study of Chinese politics, African politics, Cuban politics, Caribbean politics, etc. Area specialization further delimits a sub-field for a more concentrated analysis and survey. The area approach moves more towards a micro-analysis rather than a macro-analysis of political life. While both approaches have their merits and usefulness, the specific study of Japanese politics, for example, makes Comparative Governments and Politics more illuminating and comprehensive.

Area specialization grew slowly, and generally in a chaotic and unsystematic fashion. And it is still limited by many factors. The study and analysis of the political characteristics of a country is heavily dependent upon grants, fellowships, leaves of absence, and is hampered by language difficulties and travel restrictions, among other factors. Because of this, area studies on western countries heavily predominate to date, but activity in non-western studies is increasing, and the prospect, given today's international climate, is that many more highly specialized studies are in the offing.

But as area specialization for foreign countries grew in political science, it was slow in emerging for the United States. In this pluralist society, composed of numerous ethnic groups, several of them maintaining their own distinctions, a great opportunity went unattended. The basic reason was the notion that the U.S. was a melting-pot type of society, [2] that despite differences in ethnic background, everyone became part of one group with similar traits and therefore similar political behavior. But the ethnic and ideological protest which came in the sixties and seventies exploded the myth[3] and challenged those who had been chiefly concerned with its perpetuation in scholarly endeavors.

This new decade of the seventies saw the launching of numerous ethnic and cultural studies programs. Black studies, Mexican-American or Chicano studies grew by leaps and bounds.[4] And area specialization in political science at home emerged as a completely new potential. But no rush to create area competence and new sub-fields has emerged.

To be sure, there have been some studies and analyses of black politics but they have been mostly limited and narrow sectional surveys.[5] At the present, the political activities of black Americans have not come to be viewed as a sub-field of political science; nor have such areas of specialization as black political parties, electoral behavior, pressure group activity, etc., been undertaken.

Black politics, which has come to be defined as an attempt by Afro-Americans in the American political system to implement their preferences into public policy, is not yet a major sub-field or an area of specialization in political science. To be sure, it should be, and the many inquiries and analyses emerging or presently under way may provide the impetus and the eventual subject matter. But that is still to come; thus far, study in this field has been haphazard and unsystematic. Journalists, fly-by-night writers, novelists, travelers, observers and writers of reminiscences have provided most of what has been known heretofore about the field. The early studies were limited and have received little attention. Moreover, many of them were by white authors.[6] Works by white authors such as Paul Lewinson's

Race, Class and Party; H. D. Price's The Negro and Southern Politics; Harold Gosnell's seminal Negro Politicians;
V. O. Key's Southern Politics in State and Nation; and
Alexander Heard's A Two-Party South were the major contributions in the early thirties, forties and fifties. The
only works by black political scientists were: William F.
Nowlin, The Negro in American National Politics; Elbert
Tatum, The Changed Political Thought of the Negro, 1915-
1940, and John R. Lynch, The Facts of Reconstruction,
issued in 1913.

        The late fifties and early sixties brought such efforts
as James Q. Wilson's Negro Politics; Pat Watters' Climbing
Jacob's Ladder; Everett C. Ladd's Negro Political Leader-
ship in the South; William R. Keech's The Role of the Vote
in the Quest for Equality; Donald Matthews and James
Prothro's Negroes and the New Southern Politics; and
Negro Politics in America, edited by Harry Bailey. For the
most part these were general studies. More specialized
studies included: Hanes Walton, Jr.'s The Negro in Third
Party Politics and The Political Philosophy of Martin Luther
King; Chuck Stone's Black Political Power in America; and
Stokely Carmichael and Charles Hamilton's Black Power:
The Politics of Liberation in America.

        In the 1970's came Hanes Walton, Jr.'s Black
Politics and his specialized work, Black Political Parties.
During this period numerous readers appeared: Herbert J.
Storing's What Country Have I?: Political Writings of
Black Americans; Howard Brotz (ed), Negro Social and
Political Thought, 1850-1920; and Lenneal Henderson (ed),
Black Political Life in the United States.

        In addition, as new black politicians came to power

in the late sixties and early seventies, numerous black political autobiographies were published. Shirley Chisholm wrote Unbought and Unbossed; H. Rap Brown, Die Nigger Die; Julian Bond, A Time to Speak, A Time to Act; Floyd McKissick, Three-Fifths of a Man; and James Farmer, Freedom Now.

In short, the beginning of the seventies saw many new and useful books on black politics, and some represent serious scholarly effort. However, most of the readers, with the exception of Lenneal Henderson's volume and Senator Dymally's The Black Politician, were poor and hardly worth the reading. [7] However, they did increase access to the limited studies available and helped expand significantly the study of the field of black politics.

The proliferation of books on the subject resulted from several factors such as the black social revolution of the sixties, the collapse of the melting-pot myth, the emergence of numerous black politicians and the increase in black political scientists. [8] The last factor aided greatly because black scholars became more aware of the neglect of the political activities of blacks and many were motivated by the small but significant scholarly tradition within their black institutions to do something about the omissions and commissions of the past. [9]

Political Science in Black Education

Study of political science in black colleges began during the early forties [10] and the concern with black politics, while very small at first, increased with time and the pace of political events involving the civil rights of black Americans.

In the large black colleges political science began as
a joint department with history. In the small school it con-
sisted of only a single general education course or was a
part of the general social science curriculum. By 1968,
40 per cent of the 81 black colleges offered a degree program in political science, 17 per cent had a minor concentration program, and 43 per cent had no program at all.
In addition, until 1968, only three black colleges (Fisk,
Howard and Lincoln University of Pennsylvania) offered a
course on black politics. [11]

Noting this omission and the need for a positive
political socialization of blacks in their own colleges, Professor Jewel Prestage, Chairman of the Department of
Political Science at Southern University, with some foundation support, began a study of black colleges' political
science curricula, hoping to rearrange them to include
courses on black politics. Her efforts succeeded and over
half of the black colleges today offer some courses on the
political activities of black Americans. In addition, at the
prodding of Professor Samuel D. Cook, the Ford Foundation
set up a doctoral program at Atlanta University and en-
larged the program at Howard University, both treating
political science from a black perspective. Both programs
promise to be productive and informative and the future
graduates should tremendously increase the available data on
the politics of black Americans.

Theories of Black Politics

Since social science was developed primarily as a
scientific tool to deal with the social problems that beset
man in his human relationships, the early writing on black
politics sought in that tradition to deal with many of the

problems which menaced black-white race relations in America. [12] Most of the literature in the thirties through the sixties, with the possible exceptions of Tatum and Walton, dealt with and espoused the electoral theory of Black Politics.

The electoral theory posits that as more and more blacks become voters and participants within the political system, the problems and burdens which plague black communities as well as black-white relationships would diminish almost to the vanishing point. This electoral thesis was accepted by many and maintains a strong hold over most of the studies and literature on black political activities. Even today, the old electoral approach has been modified, remolded and pressed into service to explain contemporary black political phenomena under the rubric of coalition politics, which we shall discuss later.

As I have already indicated, not everyone accepted the thesis that a dearth of black voters was the reason for the impotence and the lack of substance of black politics. Professor Samuel D. Cook of Atlanta University, in the decade between 1955 and 1965, fought the electoral theory both implicitly and forthrightly, and thereby raised the study of black politics to a new level. Professor Cook, a well trained political scientist from Ohio State University, argued in his writing that race influenced the substance as well as the style of black political life in the south. [13] This theory of racism articulates the basic assumption that racism (black or white), not a flaw in the electoral system, prevents the realization of democracy and therefore the solution to problems that hamper improved black-white relationships and the much-in-need black community.

Cook saw racism permeating all the political institutions
of the south, thus defying and preventing the dream, promise
and spirit of a true democratic system.   Racism, as he
saw it, was the Achilles' heel of the American democratic
framework. [14]

Cook's theory of racism made it possible to drop the
emphasis upon reforming and repairing the electoral appara-
tus and to see the need for attention to the entire system.
His theory made it feasible to see the total picture, to
demonstrate the additional burdens which electoral politics
alone could not remove.   From Cook's point of view, black
politics was not only a struggle for power and the values
associated with it, but also a struggle against the conse-
quences and the impact of racism in the American democratic system.   In short, black politics had the dual task
of gaining power and destroying racism in the political
system.   However, while Cook's theory of racism was
aimed at a truly integrated society, rid of racial concern,
it did give rise to the development of the colonial analogy,
or the black nationalism theory of black politics.

The black nationalist or colonial model of black
politics began with the theory of racism, but changed the
focus of the theory.   It posits a separate or segregated
society.   As put forth by Carmichael, Hamilton, Imamu
Baraka (LeRoi Jones), Harold Cruse, et. al., [15] it argues
that white racism has removed all possibilities of reform and
equality under the present political system.   Therefore,
black people must recognize their cultural unity, their need
for power and their great destiny, and must use these
things to achieve their goal.   Black politics, as these individuals see it, is a technique to gain self-control, self-

determination and independence from the colonial masters.
For the nationalist and culturalist theorist, a pluralistic
or separatist society is the goal.   Although black nationalism has been a constant feature in black political thought,
the concept of black power did much to push it to the fore-
front and in keen competition with the old idea of integration and an integrated society.

To combat this rising theory and point of view the
liberal scholars of the sixties, both black and white, recog-
nizing that the old electoral approach was undergoing
attack, tried to resurrect and sustain it, as well as the
vision of an integrated society.

Black political activist Bayard Rustin led the way in
formulating a new electoral theory called coalition politics. [16]
The coalition theory of black politics, as advanced by Rustin
and further developed and structured by others, [17] argued
that the problem that entrapped and encircled black Americans could not be removed by blacks alone.   This theory
at once tried to refute the argument of the culturalist, the
nationalist and the colonial modelist, and advance an approach
which would solve the racial problem in America.   The
coalitionist argues that blacks and whites together, working
either on a permanent or an ad hoc basis, in an issue-to-
issue coalition--liberal whites and labor blacks, or conservative whites and blacks, or a poor white-black coalition,
or an idealogical coalition--could solve not only the ills of
the black community but those of the community and society
at large. [18]   These arguments were advanced not only by
scholars, both black and white, but also by a variety of
black politicians and by political leaders who were intent
upon maintaining the fruits of power.

At the present time the coalition theory dominates the literature on black politics and seeks to replace the position once enjoyed by the electoral theory. In essence, however, the coalition theory is a new version or up-dated version of the old electoral approach. It simply adds to the old notion that while voters can do the job, other groups must assist with their votes, under a variety of conditions and alliances. Professor Harry Holloway's book, The Politics of the Southern Negro, which appeared in 1969, was the first major work in the field to indicate that only coalition politics, and not separate and independent efforts, could be effective. After thoroughly examining one state, three countries and four cities, he concluded that "coalitions with the 'better sort of white' offer (the) best prospects of success."[19] A black political scientist, Professor Tobe Johnson, apparently unaware of the trends, theories and the basis of black politics, wrongly criticized Holloway's work[20] as lacking a meaningful methodology, a frame of reference, etc., and dismissed it as worthless. In reality, however, the work was a serious effort to look at the variety of coalitions which scholars were advancing as helpful for blacks in achieving their goals and objectives. Holloway set out to test these theories through field studies and the case study approach and to determine which seemed to be the most practical. This the book did in an admirable fashion, and while it may not be totally convincing, it did give scholars a chance to view in practice the working of black politics on several levels--state, county and municipal --and in several different states: Mississippi, Tennessee, Alabama, Georgia and Texas.

Since Holloway's ground-breaking study, and in the

publications of other authors and politicians, especially
black ones, [21] the argument for coalition politics is growing.
However, the coalition theory of black politics has not cap-
tured the allegiance of all scholars.   The development theory
of black politics goes beyond but encompasses much of the
other approaches.   The developmental theorists see institutional arrangement as being the key, and see the rise of
several stages in which major reforms and changes occur
before the final stage or ultimate goal is achieved.   The
developmentalist tries to discern each stage, argue for the
next and lay bare the problem inherent on each plateau.
Since society and its institutions undergo change and reform
in each level of development, then each stage of black
politics is progressively more beneficial and fruitful to all
involved.   While some developmental schemes allow for
reversals, the basic view is optimistic about society and
man's ability to improve.   The developmentalist sees the
problem of racism and electoral arrangement as being
solved through progress.   This theory bypasses the struggle
between the coalitionist and separatist/nationalist, seeing
each as academic but necessary at certain stages or levels
of development.   No sides are taken and the dichotomization
of means and ends is not a constant issue.   For the developmentalist, one end is all that is possible, but a variety of
means may be employed as society progresses to its final
purpose.

        A small amount of writing on black politics--Lenneal
Henderson's Black Political Life in America and Robert
Holmes' Black Politics and Public Policy--goes one step
further.   These writers argue that public policies are the
key to black politics.   This policy theory of black politics

advances the older theories, seeing the outputs of the political system as the most important point of focus. For
them, systematic, comprehensive and meaningful legislation geared towards creating a truly equal society is the
road to progress. The task of black politics, as they see
it, is to achieve the right kind of policy enactment. It is
not the institution or reform that is the major concern, although these are important; it is the policy decision that the
institution makes. If black politics can redirect or influence
the policy enactments, this becomes the most important
feature of black political activity.

Professor Mack Jones, in his "A Frame of Reference
of Black Politics,"[23] illustrated how the possibilities of
certain coalitions within policy-making institutions could
be effected to produce desired policy enactments. But he
concluded that the majority in these institutions would never
permit the minority to rise from their subordinate position.
To date, the public policy-oriented theorists have not
answered Professor Jones' criticism.

The economic (Marxist-Socialist) theory of black
politics[24] argues that it is not electoral, institutional
policy or radical developmental approaches to black politics
that best describe or offer a panacea for the plight of Black
Americans. Instead of race, the Marxian theory sees
class, or the economic structure, as being both the root of
evil and the key to black politics. As they see it--black
politics has failed in the past and will continue to fail to
solve the problems of the black community because politics,
no matter of what kind, never touches the evil of the
capitalist system: the exploitation and subjection of the
poor and the many for the benefit of the few. Professor

Mack Jones, who began by attacking the policy theorists and
their antecedents, has argued in subsequent essays that the
key role of black politics might be to teach and educate the
masses that politics will fail and that black liberation lies
outside of the political milieu. [25] For the economic theorists,
the best black politics can offer is only a temporary relief
and pacification of the masses. In other words, the
reformism of current black politics is bound to fail and is
ineffectual in alleviating the problems which beset the
masses. This constant failure of black politics will only
make the masses more revolutionary and the possibility of
a successful revolutionary overthrow of society much more
imminent. To the Marxian theorist, the new society will
be integrated, but with a much more equitable economic
system which will overcome man's alienation from his fel-
low man.

　　　This approach has not yet come to fruition. Many
of the problems--theoretical, methodological, structural
and functional--have not been worked out. While many
rising black political scientists are coming to see the influence of economics on black politics, and there have been
several works by black political observers, [26] major studies
of black politics from an economic point of view have not
yet emerged.

　　　Several economic theorists have begun to link the
black political struggle in America with that in the third
world. [27] One wing of the Black Panther Party, Professor
Angela Davis, and some of the black leaders in the communist party like Claude Lightfoot have made a beginning
in this area. But political scientists' efforts in this area
have been slow to emerge, and much of the present

literature tends to clash with the black nationalist theory
which tries to link up the black political struggle in America
and the third world, on the basis of race and nationalism
rather than on an economic basis. The constant argument
of class versus race continues, and it is this conflict which
attracts much of the energies of writers in the field, nearly
all of whom take one side or the other.

In the future, one may expect other new theories to
develop, perhaps combining elements of the old or advancing
of approaches thus far unknown (see Figure 1).

Summary and Conclusions

In sum, the current literature on black politics
reveals: 1) electoral; 2) racial; 3) coalitional; 4) nationalist;
5) developmental; 6) policy; and 7) Marxist-socialist theories
of black politics. Much of the present literature argues for
the coalitional approach, but some studies advocate the
nationalist approach. The rising economic approach promises
to be a new wave and to produce some influential literature.
Whether it will ever become the mainstream or result in
major studies remains moot, partly at least because of the
shift of major publishing houses away from that position.
This is a major obstacle at present for the economic
theorist.

One of the major problems that have plagued all of
the theoretical positions and their formulations has been the
absence of objective and systematic studies of black politics.
The late development of the field and the slow rise of area
specialization have left theorists with little basic data to
use. Most of what there is on black politics has not been
gathered and analyzed, and while the earlier studies were
sectional--dealing for example with black politics in the

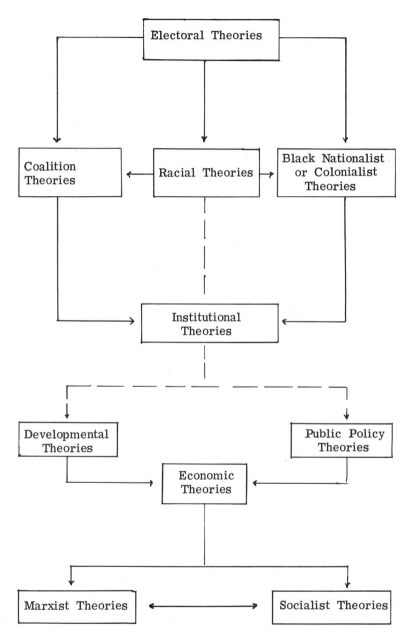

Figure 1.   Theories of Black Politics

north--the needed key works on black parties, on presidential
candidates and politics, have not emerged.

The works of Professor Hanes Walton, Jr. in the
late sixties and early seventies were steps to correct this
dearth of factual information. His first book, The Negro in
Third Party Politics, was the first work to deal systematically with blacks in the various third parties which had
appeared throughout American politics. His next work,
The Political Philosophy of Martin Luther King, Jr. was
again the first to deal in a serious and scholarly manner
with the political thought of a black leader; it attempted to
set up categories and a methodology for looking at the
political thought of other leaders. His next work, Black
Politics, tried to view, in comprehensive detail, the basic
factors and events in black political life in America from
colonial times to the present.

Walton's next book, Black Political Parties, went
into detail about the history and nature of black parties.
Again the first and only work on the subject, it contains
numerous charts, graphs, and maps, pinpointing the
travails of independent black political efforts. Some of his
new and forthcoming studies will deal with other factors of
black political life that have been little explored.

Vast areas of black politics remain, however, that
need to be studied: the problems of black legislators and
their legislation; of black judges, black politicians and
their political styles; of metro-government, political behavior, black governors and gubernatorial candidates, black
presidential candidates, [28] congressmen and congressional
candidates, electoral behavior, the role of the media,
political campaign and many other areas. As exploration

of these fields adds more data, old theories will be up-
dated or dropped, new ones formulated; new perspectives
will be gained and old positions will become indefensible.
The theories of black politics will constantly change and
grow. [29]

Heretofore there has not existed a systematic and
comprehensive bibliographic work on black politics.   Although
several works list significant bibliographies on black political activity--notably Henderson's Black Political Life in
America and Walton's Black Politics--these were not intended
to be as comprehensive as this volume attempts to be.
This book attempts to indicate the trends in the literature,
past and present interpretations of available data, some
new areas which need exploring and analyzing, and future
prospects in the field of black politics.

It is hoped that black politics will advance and become much more important in political science, and that
area specialists will soon come to include specific areas
within black politics among their competences.   The literature listed herein may serve as a guide and a stimulus
to those who will advance the frontiers of knowledge ever
further.

Notes

1.   See Albert Somit and Joseph Tannenhaus, The Develop-
      ment of American Political Science: from Burgess
      to Behavioralism (Boston: Allyn and Bacon, 1967),
      Chapter 1, and their American Political Science--
      A Profile of a Discipline (New York: Atherton
      Press, 1964).

2.   See Nathan Glazer and Daniel P. Moynihan, Beyond
      the Melting Pot (Cambridge: Harvard University
      Press, 1963).

3. Walt Anderson, The Age of Protest (California: Good-
    year Publishing Company, 1969), pp. 79-292.

4. For works on black studies see John Blassingame (ed.),
    New Perspectives on Black Studies (Urbana: Univer-
    sity of Illinois Press, 1971), and Armstead L.
    Robinson, et. al. (eds.), Black Studies in the Uni-
    versity (New Haven: Yale University, 1969).   For
    Chicano studies see, Luis Valdez and Stan Steiner
    (eds.), Aztlan: An Anthology of Mexican Literature
    (New York: Knopf, 1972), and Edward Simmen,
    Pain and Promise: the Chicano Today (Cleveland,
    New American Liberty, 1972).   For Indian studies
    see Vine Deloria, Jr., Custer Died for Your Sins
    (New York: Avon Books, 1970), and Dee Brown,
    Bury My Heart at Wounded Knee (New York,   Holt,
    Rinehart & Winston, 1971).

5. See Hanes Walton, Jr., Black Politics: A Theoretical
    and Structural Analysis (Philadelphia: J. B. Lippin-
    cott, 1972).

6. Ibid., p. 5-8.

7. On this point, see C. Vernon Gray, Leslie McLemore
    and Hanes Walton, Jr., "Black Politics: The
    View from the Readers," American Politics (January,
    1973).

8. Lenneal Henderson, "Engineers of Black Liberation,"
    Black Politician (April, 1970) pp. 12-16.   See also
    J. Prestage, "Report of the Conference on Political
    Service Curriculum at Predominantly Black Institu-
    tions," P.S. (Summer, 1969) pp. 322-336.

9. See John Hope Franklin, "The Dilemma of the Black
    Scholar," in Herbert Hill (ed.), Soon One Morning
    (New York: Knopf, 1963).

10. See Twiley Barker,   "Political Science in Institutions
    of Higher Learning for Negroes; Some Observations
    on Departmental Organization and Curriculum,"
    Quarterly Review of Higher Education Among
    Negroes (July, 1959), pp. 139-148.   See also
    Merze Tate, "The Teaching of International Rela-
    tions in Negro Colleges," Ibid (July, 1947), pp.
    149-154.

11. See Hanes Walton, Jr. and Brenda D. Mobley, "Polit-
     ical Science Education in the Black College, " Ap-
     pendix II in this volume.

12. On this point, see Hanes Walton, Jr., "The Race Rela-
     tions Courses in Black Colleges, " Negro Educational
     Review (October, 1968) pp. 123-132.

13. For this argument, which Professor Cook has put forth
     again and again in many of his writings, see Samuel
     Cook, "Political Organization and Movements in the
     South, " Journal of Politics (February, 1964); and
     his "The Key to Southern Liberation...," Conference
     Proceedings: Southwide Conference of Black Elected
     Officials (Atlanta: Southern Regional Council, 1968).

14. Samuel D. Cook, "The American Liberal Democratic
     Tradition, the Black Revolution, and Martin Luther
     King, Jr., " in H. Walton, Jr., The Political
     Philosophy of Martin Luther King, Jr. (Conn.:
     Greenwood, 1971.)

15. See Charles Hamilton and Stokely Carmichael, Black
     Power: The Politics of Liberation in America (New
     York: Random House, 1967); and Floyd Barbour
     (ed.), The Black Power Revolt (Boston: Porter
     Sargent, 1969).

16. See Bayard Rustin "From Protest to Politics, the
     Refute of the Civil Rights Movement, " Commentary
     (February, 1964), and his "Black Power and
     Coalition Politics, " Ibid., (February 1965).

17. For a complete list, see Prestage, "Black Politics..."
     Social Science Quarterly (Dec., 1968), p. 463.

18. For the first systematic analysis of the numerous
     coalition theories and arguments for black politics,
     see Hanes Walton, Jr., Black Coalitional Politics
     (forthcoming).

19. Harry Holloway, The Politics of the Southern Negro
     (New York: Random House, 1969), p. 345.

20. Tobe Johnson, "Review of The Politics of the Southern
     Negro by Harry Holloway, " American Political
     Science Review, (March, 1970), pp. 196-97.

21. Hanes Walton, Jr. and Isaiah McIver, "Black Political
     Autobiographies: Panaceas for a Race," Journal of
     Ethnic Studies (forthcoming).

22. Prestage, op. cit. p. 462-465.

23. Henderson, op. cit.

24. See Edward Greer, Black Liberation Politics: A
     Reader (Boston: Allyn and Bacon, 1971).

25. See Mack H. Jones, The Responsibility of Black
     Political Scientists to the Black Community (1971);
     Government Structure and Urban Policy (1972);
     Blacks and Politics in Atlanta: Myth and Reality:
     1972.

26. See James Boggs, Racism and the Class Struggle
     (New York: Monthly Review Press, 1970).

27. Angela Davis, If They Came in The Morning (New
     York: New American Library, 1971).

28. For the lead work in this area, see Hanes Walton,
     Jr. and Ronald Clark, "Black Presidential Candi-
     dates: Past and Present," New South (Spring,
     1972), pp. 14-22.

29. For an even newer approach, see H. Walton, Jr.,
     The Poetry of Black Politics (London: Regency
     Press, 1972).

Chapter II

BLACK POLITICAL SOCIALIZATION

Political socialization is the way society transmits its political culture from generation to generation. The process may serve to preserve existing political norms, or may act as a vehicle for social and political change.

The articles and books listed within this section tend to describe the agencies and how they influence the socialization process within the black community. Professor Jewel Prestage of Southern University has done the greatest amount of study in this area, but as of this writing none of her work has been published.

What literature does exist offers excellent insights for the beginner and the scholar, and provides many points of departure for further study. The general trend of this literature is toward the position that all existing agencies have tended to teach blacks non-political involvement because this was what the majority of the political culture wanted. Professor Prestage indicates that the majority of researchers working the area of political socialization deliberately left out blacks. As for data on how to reverse this trend and re-focus researchers--there is none.

Looking at the agencies within the black community, the black church appears to be most significant. During the decade of the sixties the church has moved many blacks from non-involvement to involvement.

CHURCH

Articles

Cone, James H.   "Failure of the Black Church, " Liberation
        (May 1969), 15-17+.

Elder, John Dixon.   "Meeting the Crisis of Negro Leader-
        ship in the Church, " Harvard Divinity Bulletin, I
        (Autumn 1967), 17-18.

Fleming, G. James.   "The Negro Church and Politics, "
        Risk Magazine, Geneva, Switzerland, 1967.

Hatchett, John F.   "The Moslem Influence Among American
        Negroes, " Journal of Human Relations, X (Summer,
        1962), 375-380.

Moss, James A.   "The Negro Church and Black Power, "
        Journal of Human Relations, 17 (First Quarter, 1968),
        119-128.

Muhammad, Elijah.   "What the Black Muslims Believe, "
        Negro Digest, XIII (November, 1963).

"Negro Minister Visits Russia, " Ebony, XI, No. 1 (Novem-
        ber 1955), 200.

Wood, James R.   "The Churches and Civil Rights, " Ameri-
        can Sociological Review, 35 (August, 1970).

Dissertations

Carter, Luther C. , Jr.   Negro Churches in a Southern
        Community.   Yale University, 1955.

Fredericks, David.   The Role of the Negro Minister in
        New Orleans Politics.   Tulane University, 1967.

Gilman, Martin.   Adat Boyt Moshe--The Colored House of
        Moses: A Study of a Contemporary Negro Religious
        Community and Its Leader.   University of Pennsyl-
        vania, 1965.

Howard, John R.   Becoming a Black Muslim: A Study of
        Commitment Processes in a Deviant Political Organ-
        ization.   Stanford University, 1965.

Jenkins, John J. The Structure and Function of the American Negro Church in Race Integration. Boston University, 1952.

Johnstone, Ronald L. Militant and Conservative Community Leadership Among Negro Clergymen. University of Michigan, 1963.

Reimers, David M. Protestant Churches and the Negro: A Study of Several Major Protestant Denominations and the Negro from World War One to 1954. University of Wisconsin, 1961.

Books

Cleage, Albert B., Jr. The Black Messiah. New York: Sheed and Ward, 1968.

Cone, James H. Black Theology and Black Power. New York: The Seabury Press, 1969.

Epps, Archie. The Speeches of Malcolm X at Harvard. New York: William Morrow and Company, Inc., 1968.

Fauset, Arthur H. Black Gods of the Metropolis. Philadelphia: University of Pennsylvania Press, 1944.

Frazier, E. Franklin. The Negro Church in America. New York: Schocken, 1963.

Hamilton, Charles. The Black Preacher in America. New York: Morrow, 1972.

Kittagawa, Daisuke. The Pastor and the Race Issue. New York: Seabury Press, 1965.

Lincoln, C. Eric. The Black Muslims in America. Boston: Beacon Press, 1964.

Leonard, Joseph T. Theology and Race Relations. Milwaukee: Bruce Publishing Company, 1963.

Malcolm X. Malcolm X Speaks: Selected Speeches and Statements. Edited by George Breitman. New York: Merit Publishers, 1965.

Mays, Benjamin E. and Joseph W. Nicholson. The Negro's
     Church. New York: Institute of Social and Religious
     Research, 1933.

Moellering, Ralph. Christian Conscience and Negro Emanci-
     pation. Philadelphia: Fortress Press, 1965.

Poole, Elijah (Elijah Muhammad). Message to the Black
     Man in America. Chicago: Muhammad Mosque of
     Islam No. 2, 1965.

Ramsey, Paul. Christian Ethics and the Sit-in. New York:
     Association Press, 1961.

Sellus, James E. The South and Christian Ethics. New
     York: Association Press, 1962.

Washington, Joseph R. Black Religion: The Negro and Chris-
     tianity in the United States. Boston: Beacon Press,
     1964.

_____. The Politics of God. Boston: Beacon Press, 1967.

SCHOOLS

Articles

Ashmore, Harry S. "The Negro and the Schools," American
     Journal of Sociology, 604-605.

Billings, Charles E. "The Political Socialization of High
     School Black Activists," in Byron Massialas, Political
     Youth, Traditional Schools. Englewood Cliffs, N.J.:
     Prentice-Hall, 1972.

Bond, Horace M. "Education for Political and Social Re-
     sponsibility: Its Natural History in the American
     Colleges," Journal of Negro Education, XVI (Spring,
     1947), 165-171.

Prestage, Jewel Limar. "The Social Studies and Political
     Education," Journal of Louisiana Education Association
     (November 1964).

Singletary, James D. "Teacher--Administrative Leader Per-
     ceptions of Pupils," Journal of Educational Research,
     45 (October 1951).

BLACK PERSONALITY

Articles

Marvick, Dwaine. "The Political Socialization of the American Negro," The Annals, CCCIX (September, 1965).

Olsen, Marvin E. "Social and Political Participation of Blacks," American Sociological Review, 35 (August, 1970), 682-696.

Seasholes, Bradbury. "Political Socialization of Negroes: Image Development of Self and Politics," in William Kvaraceus, et. al. (ed.), Negro Self-Concept (New York: McGraw-Hill Book Company, 1965).

Sharma, Mehan Lal. "Martin Luther King: Modern America's Greatest Theologian of Social Action," Journal of Negro History, LIII, No. 3 (July, 1968).

Smythe, Hugh H. and James A. Moss. "The Negro Church and Black Power," Journal of Human Relations, XVII (Fall, 1969), 119-127.

Chapter III

BLACKS AND THE MAJOR POLITICAL PARTIES

Political parties are endemic to the American political process and provide the political system with a mechanism whereby peaceful political change can occur. However, political parties in America have suffered from racism and from the economic influence of the rich. The literature below describes the role, influence and participation of blacks in the major and minor parties.

Some of the literature also describes, catalogues, and analyzes the efforts of blacks to go beyond the major and minor parties by creating new independent political parties of their own. These black parties, being either of the separate or independent type (i.e., not affiliated with either one of the major parties or with minor parties--like the Negro Protective Party, the Afro-American Party and the Black Panther Party) or of the satellite or parallel type (i.e., affiliated with one of the major parties--like the Mississippi Freedom Democratic Party, the National Democratic Party of Alabama, or the numerous Black and Tan Republican Parties), have all had some influence and impact on the political process. They have played a major role in black political activities, but have since been mostly ignored or forgotten.

GENERAL

Articles

Lachman, Seymour P. "Political Parties, Intergroup Relations and Democracy," Journal of Human Relations,
XIII (Fall, 1965), 7-12.

LeCount, Louis K. "Party Affiliation in Negro Harlem,"
Opportunity, XI (April, 1933).

Matthews, Donald and James W. Prothre. "Southern Images
of Political Parties: A Comparison of White and Negro
Attitudes," Journal of Politics, XXVI (February, 1964),
82-111.

Wilkins, Roy. "Two Political Parties and the Negro Vote,"
McCall's, 92 (November, 1964), 30.

BLACKS AND THE REPUBLICAN PARTY

Articles

Baker, V. S. "Black Americans Want In: Negroes and the
GOP," National Review Bulletin, 22 (August 25, 1970),
892-893.

Booker, Simeon. "What Republicans Must Do to Regain
Negro Vote," Ebony, XVII, No. 6 (April, 1962), 47-55.

_____. "What the GOP Victory Means for Negroes,"
Ebony, XXII, No. 4 (February, 1967), 88-94.

Cox, Lawanda and John H. "Negro Suffrage and Republican
Politics: The Problem of Motivation in Reconstruction
Historiography," Journal of Southern History, XXXVIII
(August, 1967), 303-330.

DeSantis, Vincent. "Negro Dissatisfaction with Republican
Policy in the South, 1882-1884," Journal of Negro History, XXVI (April 1951), 144-155.

_____. "The Republican Party and the Southern Negro,"
Journal of Negro History (April, 1960), 71-88.

DuBois, W. E. B. "The Republican and the Black Voter,"

The Nation, CXI (June 6, 1920), 757-759.

Gelb, Joyce. "Black Republicans in New York, A Minority
    Group in a Minority." A paper presented at the 54th
    Annual Meeting of the Association for the Study of
    Negro Life and History in Birmingham (October 16,
    1968).

Katznelson, Ira. "The Politics of Race in New York City,
    1900-1930; a Taste of Honey," A paper presented at
    the 54th Annual Meeting of the Association for the
    Study of Negro Life and History, Birmingham (October
    10, 1969).

King, Mary. "The Republican Party and the Emancipation
    Proclamation," Journal of Negro History, XLVIII (April,
    1963), 98-114.

"Negroes Swing: Experts Forecast Their Return to the Re-
    publican Fold in 1940," Newsweek, 13 (April 10, 1939),
    15.

Riddleberger, Patrick W. "The Break in the Radical Ranks:
    Liberals v. Stalwarts in the Election of 1872."
    Journal of Negro History, XLIV (April 1959), 136-157.

Russ, William Jr. "The Negro and White Disfranchisement
    During Radical Reconstruction," Journal of Negro His-
    tory, XLIV (April, 1959), 136-157.

Sherman, Richard B. "Republicans and Negroes: The Lessons
    of Normalcy," Phylon (First Quarter, 1956).

"6,000,000 Negro Votes: A Decisive Bloc. Will They Return
    to the GOP," Newsweek, 47 (April 9, 1956), 33-35.

"Strange Political Bedfellows: Republican-Dixiecrat Coalition,"
    Negro History Bulletin, 16 (November, 1952), 48.

Walton, Hanes Jr. "The Politics of the Black and Tan Repub-
    licans." A paper presented at the 54th Annual Meeting
    of the Association for the Study of Negro Life and His-
    tory in Birmingham (October 10, 1969).

Books

Cosman, Bernard. Republicanism in the Metropolitan South.
    University: University of Alabama Press, 1960.

Heard, Alexander. A Two-Party South. Chapel Hill: Universi-
    ty of North Carolina Press, 1952.

Hirshson, Stanley P. Farewell to the Bloody Shirts: Northern
    Republicans and the Southern Negro, 1877-1893.
    Bloomington: Indiana University Press, 1962.

Logan, Rayford W. The Betrayal of the Negro. New York:
    Collier Books, 1965.

Quarles, Benjamin. Lincoln and the Negro. New York:
    Oxford University Press, 1962.

Walton, Hanes. Black Republicans: The Politics of the
    Black & Tans (Forthcoming).

BLACKS AND THE DEMOCRATIC PARTY

Articles

Abrams, Ray H. "The Copperhead Newspapers and the
    Negro," Journal of Negro History, XX (April, 1935),
    131-152.

Allswang, John. "The Chicago Negro Voter and the Demo-
    cratic Consensus: A Case Study, 1918-1936," in
    Bernard Sternsher (ed.), The Negro in Depression and
    War (Chicago: Quadrangle Books, 1969), 234-252.

Bendiner, Robert. "Negro Vote and the Democrats," The
    Reporter, 14 (May 31, 1956), 8-12.

Bode, K. "Blacks, Democrats and the '72 Convention,"
    New Republic, 65 (October 16, 1971), 11-15.

Brewer, James H. "Robert Lee Van, Democrat or Republi-
    can: An Exponent of Loose Leaf Politics," Negro His-
    tory Bulletin, XXI (February, 1958), 100-103.

Broderick, Francis L. "DuBois and the Democratic Party,
    1908-1916," Negro History Bulletin, XXI (November,
    1957), 41-46.

"Democrats and the Negro Vote," New Republic, III (Aug. 7, 1944).

Fishel, Leslie. "The Negro in the New Deal Era," in Ber-
    nard Sternsher (ed.), The Negro in Depression and War
    (Chicago: Quadrangle Books, 1969), 7-28.

Fuller, Helen. "Civil Rights Split the Democrats," New Re-
    public, 118 (March 8, 1948), 16.

Lubell, Samuel. "The Negro and the Democratic Coalition,"
    Commentary, XXXVIII (August, 1964), 18-27.

Marshall, Thurgood. "The Rise and Collapse of the 'White
    Democratic Party'," Journal of Negro Education, XXVII
    (Summer 1957), 249-254.

Meier, August. "The Negro and the Democratic Party, 1875-
    1915," Phylon, XVII (Second Quarter, 1956), 173-191.

Moon, Henry Lee. "Negro Break Away from the Democrats,"
    New Republic, 135 (December 3, 1956), 17.

Piven, F. F. and Cloward, R. A. "Dissensus Politics;
    Negroes and the Democratic Coalition," New Republic,
    158 (April 20, 1968), 20-24.

                        BLACK PARTIES

Articles

Analavage, Robert. "Lowndes Party Girds for Future," The
    Southern Patriot (December, 1966).

_____. "A Victory in Defeat in Lowndes," National Guardi-
    an (November 19, 1966).

"The Case for an Independent Black Political Party." Inter-
    national Socialist Review, 29 (January-February, 1968),
    39-55.

Clarke, John Henrik. "Black Power and Blacks," Negro
    Digest, XVIII (February 1969), 13-20.

"Congressional Challenge: Mississippi Freedom Democratic
    Party's Efforts to Remove Mississippi's Five Congress-
    men from their Seats in the House," Commonweal, 81
    (January 22, 1965), 532.

DeBerry, Clyde E. "Black Power and Black Population: A Dilemma," Journal of Negro Education, XXXVIII (Winter, 1969).

"Freedom Party Enters Race," New York Times (June 1, 1966), 34.

Gether, Solomon. "Black Power: Three Years Later," Negro Digest, XIX (December, 1969).

Guyot, Lawrence and Thelwell, Mike. "The Politics of Necessity and Survival in Mississippi," Freedomways (Spring, 1966), 120-132.

Herbers, John. "Mississippi Freedom Democrats to Run Own Slate for Congress," New York Times Supplement (September 23, 1965), 1.

Johnson, Dorothy. "The U.C.P." Master's thesis, Columbia University.

Jones, David R. "Negro Party Puts Strength to Test," New York Times (October 4, 1964), 70.

Kifner, John. "Freedom Party Endorses Candidates," New York Times (July 22, 1968), 27.

Kopkind, Andrew. "Lair of the Black Panther: Lowndes County Negroes Form Political Party in Alabama," New Republic, 155 (August 13, 1966), 10-13.

_____. "The Future of Black Power," New Republic (January 7, 1967).

Lee, John. "Black Panthers to Oppose Powell," New York Times (July 28, 1968), 41.

McLemore, Leslie B. "The Freedom Democratic Party and the Changing Political Status of the Negro in Mississippi." Unpublished Master's thesis, Atlanta University, 1965.

Minnis, Jack. "The Mississippi Freedom Democratic Party," Freedomways, V (Spring, 1965), 264-278.

"The Mississippi Freedom Vote," New South (December 1963), 10-13.

"A Negro Party," Crisis (October, 1916).

"Negro Party Flies in Michigan," New York Times (May 3, 1964), 70.

Newton, Huey P. "The Black Panthers," Ebony, XXIV, No. 10 (August 1969), 106-112.

Rogers, William. "The Negro Alliance in Alabama," Journal of Negro History, XLV (January, 1960), 38-44.

Romaine, Anne Cook. "The Mississippi Freedom Democratic Party through 1964." Unpublished M.A. thesis, University of Virginia, 1969.

"Test for Black Power: Lowndes County Alabama," Newsweek, 68 (November 7, 1966), 37.

Thomas, Norman. "The Future of the Black Vote," Crisis, XXXVIII (February 1931), 45.

Walton, Hanes Jr. "The Negro in the Prohibition Party" (tentative title), Papers and Proceedings of the Association for the Study of Negro Life and History, Vol. 1.

Worthy, William. "An All Black Party," Liberation (October 1963).

Wright, R. R. "A Negro Party," Christian Records (October 1916).

Books

Carmichael, Stokely, and John Hulett. The Black Panther Party. New York: Merit Publishers, 1966.

The Case for a Black Party. New York. Socialist Workers Party, 1968.

Walton, Hanes, Jr. Black Political Parties: A Historical and Political Analysis. New York: Free Press, 1972.

BLACKS AND THIRD PARTIES

Articles

Abramowitz, Jack. "The Negro in the Populist Movement, "
Journal of Negro History, XXXVIII (July 1953), 257-
289.

Addams, Jane. "The Progressive Party and the Negro, "
Crisis, V (November, 1912), 30-31.

Andrews, E. F. "Socialism and the Negro." International
Socialist Review (March 1905), 254-256.

Barnes, Elizabeth. "Independent Politics: The Significance
of the Black Panther Party, " Young Socialist (October
13, 1966).

Chafe, William H. "The Negro and Populism: A Kansas
Case Study, " Journal of Southern History, 34 (August
1968), 402-419.

Crosswaith, Frank A. "The Negro Program of the Socialists, Crisis, XXXVIII (September 1931), 279-280.

Crowe, Charles. "Racial Violence and Social Reform
Origins of the Atlantic Riot of 1906, " Journal of
Negro History, LIII No. 3 (July, 1968).

_____. "Tom Watson, Populists and Blacks Recon-
sidered, " Journal of Negro History, LV, No. 2
(April, 1970).

Debs, Eugene V. "The Negro in the Class Struggle, "
The International Socialist, IV (November, 1903),
257-260.

Foner, Eric. "Politics and Prejudices: The Free Soil
Party and the Negro 1849-1852, " Journal of Negro
History, L (October 1965), 239-258.

Goodwyn, Lawrence C. "Populist Dreams and Negro Rights:
East Texas as a Case Study, " American Historical

Review, 76 (December, 1971), 1435-1456.

Grantham, Dewey W. Jr.   "The Progressive Movement and
    the Negro, " in Charles Wynes (ed.), The Negro in the
    South Since 1865 (New York: Harper, Colophon Book,
    1965), 62-82.

Gutman, Herbert.   "Peter H. Clark: Pioneer Negro
    Socialist, 1877, " Journal of Negro Education, XXXIV
    (Fall, 1965), 413-418.

Guyot, Lawrence and Mike Thelwell.   "Toward Independent
    Political Power, " Freedomways, VI (Summer, 1966),
    246-254.

Haynes, James.   "Why the Negro Should Be a Progressive, "
    Crisis, V (November, 1912), 42.

James, Daniel.   "Cannon the Progressive, " New Republic,
    CXIX (October 18, 1948), 14-15.

Miller, Loren.   "One Way Out--Communism, " Opportunity,
    XII (July, 1934).

"The New Party's Future, " New Republic, 119 (July 26, 1948).
    15.

Ranson, Reverdy C.   "Socialism and the Negro, " Alex-
    ander's Magazine, I (May 15, 1905), 15-16.

Record, Wilson.   "The Development of the Communist Posi-
    tion on the Negro Question in the United States, "
    Phylon, XIX (Fall, 1958), 306-326.

Reddick, Jamie.   "The Negro and the Populist Movement in
    Georgia. " Unpublished Master's Thesis, Atlanta
    University, 1937.

Robinson, W., Jr.   "Democratic Frontiers, " Journal of
    Human Relations (Spring, 1954), 63-70.

Roosevelt, T.   "Progressives and the Colored Man, "
    Outlook, 101 (August 24, 1912), 909-912.

Saunders, Robert.   "Southern Populists and the Negro,
    1893-1905, " Journal of Negro History, LIV, No. 3
    (July, 1969).

Smith, Asbury. "What Can the Negro Expect from Communism?" Opportunity, XI (July, 1933), 211-212.

"Socialism and the Negro Movement," Monthly Review (September, 1963).

Taylor, Joseph H. "Populism and Disfranchisement in Alabama," Journal of Negro History, XXXIV (October, 1949), 410-424.

"The Third Party and the Negro," Negro History Bulletin, XI (March, 1948), 122, 143.

Thomas, Jay. "Negro-White Unity and the Communists," Political Affairs, 46 (May, 1967), 49-54.

Thomas, Norman. "Socialism's Appeal to Negroes," Crisis, XLIII (October, 1936), 294-295.

_____. "Socialist Way Out for the Negro," Journal of Negro History, XXI (January, 1936), 100-104.

Van Zanten, John W. "Communist Theory and the Negro Question," Review of Politics, 29 (October, 1967), 435-456.

Vichini, Eraste. "Negro Locals," International Socialists Review, V (January, 1905), 389.

Wallace, Henry. "Third Parties and the American," New Republic, 118 (January 19, 1948), 12.

Walton, Hanes Jr. "Another Force for Disfranchisement: Blacks and the Prohibitionists in Tennessee," Journal of Human Relations, XVIII (Fall, 1970).

_____. "Blacks and Conservative Political Movements," Quarterly Review of Higher Education Among Negroes, XXXVII (October, 1969).

_____. "Blacks and the 1968 Third Parties," Negro Educational Review, XXI (April, 1970), 19-23.

_____. "The Negro in Early Third-Party Movements," The Negro Educational Review, XIX (April-July, 1968).

_____ . "The Negro in the Progressive Party Movements,"
Quarterly Review of Higher Education Among Negroes,
XXXVI (January, 1968).

_____ . "The Negro in the Prohibition Party: A Case
Study of the Tennessee Prohibition Party" (tentative-
ly titled), Papers and Proceedings of the 53rd Annual
Meeting of the Association for the Study of Negro Life
and History, vol. 8, 1-5.

_____ , and James E. Taylor. "Blacks, the Prohibitionists and Disfranchisement," Quarterly Review of
Higher Education Among Negroes, XXXVII (April,
1969), 65-69.

Wesley, Charles H.   "The Participation of Negroes in the
Anti-Slavery Political Parties," Journal of Negro
History, XXVI (January, 1961), 39-76.

Williams, Samuel W.   "The People's Progressive Party of
Georgia," Phylon, X (Third Quarter, 1949), 226-230.

Wolgemuth, Kathleen L.   "Woodrow Wilson's Appointment
Policy and the Negro," Journal of Southern History,
24 (November, 1958), 457-471.

Woodward, C. Vann.   "Tom Watson and the Negro in
Agrarian Politics," Journal of Southern History
(1938), 14-33.

Wright, R. R.   "A Negro Party," Christian Record
(October, 1916).

Books

Ford, James.   The Negro and the Democratic Front.   New
York: International Publishers, 1937.

More, Richard B.   Afro-Americans and the Third Party
Movement.   New York: Holt, Rinehart and Winston,
1969.

Nolan, William A.   Communism Versus the Negro.
Chicago: Henry Regnery Company, 1951.

Record, Wilson.   Race and Radicalism: The NAACP and

the Communist Party in Conflict.   Ithaca: Cornell
University Press, 1964.

_____ .   The Negro and the Communist Party.   Chapel
Hill: University of North Carolina Press, 1951.

Walton, Hanes, Jr.   The Negro in Third Party Politics.
Philadelphia: Dorrance, 1969.

Chapter IV

THE BLACK VOTE AND NATIONAL ELECTIONS

The influence and impact of the black electorate in national elections has been a major concern since the publication of Henry L. Moon's Balance of Power: The Negro Vote, in 1948. The book argued that black people held the political power to determine the outcome of most presidential elections. With a good insight into political history and with some census data, Moon showed that blacks, because of their migration northward, had come to be strategically placed in those key urban areas of the north which have the largest number of votes in the electoral college.

Moon's book set off a rush of analysts seeking either to prove or disprove his thesis. The work was a boon to the electoral theory of black politics. Moon himself produced several essays after the book which further expanded upon and validated his theories. Then, in 1968, Chuck Stone, in Black Political Power in America, challenged the thesis and provided data indicating that in some elections the presidential candidate could win without the black vote. He pointed, for example, to the Johnson landslide in 1964.

In 1968, Nixon put together a southern strategy and won without the black vote. Thus, the old Balance of Power thesis has come under attack. Recent essays point out new patterns and trends.

Articles

Andrews, M. P. "Lincoln and the Negro," Nation, 88
    (March 18, 1909), 277.

Armistead, Scott Pride. "The Negro Vote: Ike or Adlai?"
    The Nation, 175 (August 16, 1962), 124-126.

Bage, Elvena S. "President Garfield's Forgotten Pronounce-
    ment," Negro History Bulletin (June, 1951), 195-197.

Bethune, Mary McCloud. "My Secret Talks with FDR,"
    Ebony (April, 1949), 42-51.

"Black Justice; Excluding the Negro from Democratic Pri-
    mary," Nation, 140 (May 1, 1935), 497.

Blumenthal, Henry. "Woodrow Wilson and the Race Ques-
    tion," Journal of Negro History, XLVIII (January,
    1963), 1-21.

Booker, Simeon. "What Negroes Can Expect from Ken-
    nedy," Ebony, XVI, No. 3 (January, 1961), 33-38.

Brisbane, R. H. "The Negro Vote as a Balance of Power
    in the National Election," Quarterly Review of High-
    er Education Among Negroes, XX (July, 1952), 97-
    100.

Brown, Earl. "How the Negro Voted in the Presidential
    Election," Opportunity, XIV (December, 1936), 359-
    361.

_____. "The Negro Vote," Opportunity, XIV (October,
    1936), 302-304.

_____. "Negro Vote, 1944: A Forecast," Harper's
    Magazine, 185 (July, 1944), 152.

Carter, Elmer A. "How the Negro Should Vote," Opportunity,
    X (March, 1932).

_____. "The Negro Democratic Primaries," Opportunity,
    X (June, 1932).

_____. "The Negro Vote," Opportunity, X (July, 1931).

_____. "The Negro Vote," Opportunity, XIV (September, 1936).

_____. "The Negro Vote in November," Opportunity, X (March, 1932).

Collins, E. M. "Cincinnati Negroes and Presidential Politics," in Bernard Sternsher, The Negro in Depression and War (New York: Quadrangle, 1969), 258-265.

"Delicate Aspect: Southern Negroes and the New Deal," Time, 35 (September 19, 1938), 12.

Ferguson, Harold B. Jr. "Race as a Factor in Presidential Campaigns from 1904 to 1928 in North Carolina" Unpublished Master's Thesis, North Carolina College, 1949.

Gatewood, Willard B. "Theodore Roosevelt and the Indianola Affair," Journal of Negro History, LIII, No. 1 (January, 1968).

Goodman, James. "FDR New Deal: A Political Disaster for Blacks," The Black Politician (October, 1969), 33-36.

Hainsworth, Robert W. "The Negro and the Texas Primaries," Journal of Negro History, XVIII (October, 1933), 426-450.

Harrell, James A. "Negro Leadership in the Election Year 1936," Journal of Southern History, XXXIV (November, 1968), 546-565.

Harris, E. A. "Negro Faces November," New Republic, III (August 28, 1944), 241-243.

Higgs, William Leon. "LBJ and the Negro Vote: Case of the Missing Registrars," The Nation, 201 (December 13, 1965), 460-462.

"How Kennedy's Concern for the Negro Led to His Death," Ebony, XXII, No. 6 (April, 1967).

"How will Negroes Vote," Life, 17 (October 16, 1944), 89-95.

Korngold, Ralph. "Was Lincoln Really the Negro's Friend?"

Negro Digest, VIII (June, 1950).

Link, A. S. "The Negro as a Factor in the Campaign of
    1912," Journal of Negro History, XXXII (January,
    1947), 81-89.

Middleton, Russell. "The Civil Rights Issue and Presi-
    dential Voting Among Southern Negroes and Whites,"
    Social Forces, XL (March, 1962), 209-215.

Miller, J. Erroll. "The Negro in National Politics in
    1968," In P. Romero (ed.), in Black America
    (Washington, D.C.: United Publishing Corporation,
    1969), 3-40.

_____. "Philadelphia Negroes in the Roosevelt Elections,"
    The Midwest Journal (Summer, 1950).

Miller, Kenneth. "How a Negro was Elected President?"
    Negro Digest, VII (November, 1948).

Moon, Henry Lee. "How the Negro Voted," The Nation,
    159 (November 25, 1944), 640-641.

_____. "The Negro Vote in the Presidential Election of
    1956," Journal of Negro Education, XXVII (Summer,
    (19).

"The Negro Prefers Truman," New Republic, 119 (Novem-
    ber 22, 1948), 8.

"Nixon and the Negroes," Newsweek, 72 (December 30,
    1968), 20-21.

Overacker, Louise. "The Negro's Struggle for Participa-
    tion in Primary Elections," Journal of Negro History,
    XXX (January 1945), 54-61.

"The President and the Negro," Nation, 97 August 7, 1913),
    114.

Rowan, Carl T. "Harry Truman and the Negro," Ebony,
    XV, No. 1 (November, 1959), 44.

_____. "Who Will Get the Negro Vote?" Ebony, XVI,
    No. 1 (November, 1960), 40-49.

Sanders, Charles L. "The President Who Hurt Negroes
    Most," Ebony, XIX, No. 7 (May, 1964), 110.

Scammon, Richard M. "How the Negroes Voted," New
    Republic (November 21, 1960), 8-9.

Scheiner, Seth M. "President Theodore Roosevelt and the
    Negro, 1901-1908," Journal of Negro History,
    XLVII (July, 1962), 169-182.

Schouler, J. "President Johnson and Negro Suffrage,"
    Outlook, 82 (January 7, 1906), 69-73.

Sherman, Richard B. "The Harding Administration and the
    Negro: An Opportunity Lost," Journal of Negro
    History, XLIX (July, 1964), 151-168.

Strange, D. C. "Making of a President, 1912: the Northern
    Negro's View," Negro History Bulletin, 31 (Novem-
    ber, 1968), 14-23.

Sullivan, L. "Negro Vote," Atlantic Monthly, 166 (October,
    1940), 477-484.

Wesley, Charles H. "Lincoln's Plan for Colonizing the
    Emancipated Negroes," Journal of Negro History,
    IV (January, 1919), 7-21.

"What Negroes Can Expect from Lyndon B. Johnson,"
    Ebony, XIX, No. 3 (January, 1964), 81.

White, T. H. "Negro Voter, Can He Elect a President?"
    Collier's, 138 (August 17, 1956), 19-21.

White, Walter. "Will the Negro Elect the Next President?"
    Colliers, CXX (November 22, 1947), 26, 70-71.

_____. "Will the Negro Elect the Next President?"
    Negro Digest, XIII (March, 1964).

_____. "Will the Negro Elect Our Next President."
    Collier's, 120 (November 22, 1947), 26.

_____. "Will the Negro Elect the Next President?"
    Negro Digest, VI (March, 1948).

Wolgemuth, Kathleen L. "Woodrow Wilson and Federal

Segregation," Journal of Negro History, XLIV (April, 1959), 158-173.

Books

Golden, Harry.   Mr. Kennedy and the Negroes.   Cleveland: World Publishing Company, 1964.

Nowlin, William F.   The Negro in American National Politics (1868-1930).   Boston: Stratford, 1931.

Chapter V

BLACK PRESSURE GROUPS:
STATE AND LOCAL LEVELS

For years, the major black protest organizations
were considered civil rights groups and much of the literature views them from this perspective. More recent analyses have looked at these organizations more as pressure
groups, a viewpoint which has brought to light more information about the organizations' political and other activities.

In many instances, black civil rights organizations did
much more than just try to advance the cause for equality.
But these other activities rarely came into view because of
the earlier literature's over-riding concern with their civil
rights activities.

The new emphasis on the black organizations as
pressure and interest groups within the political process
should foster greater understanding of the range and objectives of these organizations.

Articles and Dissertations

Abramowitz, Jack. "Agrarian Reformers and the Negro
    Question," Negro History Bulletin, XI (March,
    1948), 138.

Anglin, Robert. "A Sociological Analysis of the NAACP."
    Unpublished Ph.D. dissertation, Indiana University,
    1950.

Aptheker, Herbert. "Militant Abolitionists," Journal of
    Negro History, XXV, No. 4 (October, 1941).

_____ . "South Carolina Negro Conventions," Journal of
Negro History, XXXI (October, 1946), 91-97.

Bailey, Harry A. Jr. "Negro Interest Group Strategies,"
Urban Affairs Quarterly (September, 1968).

Baker, A. W. "First International Congress on the Negro,
Tuskegee, 1912," Missionary Review of the World,
35 (June, 1912), 440-442.

Barnes, Johnny W. "The Political Activities of the Union
League of America in North Carolina," Quarterly
Review of Higher Education Among Negroes, XX
(October, 1952), 141-150.

Becker, H. "The Nature and Consequence of Black Propaganda, "American Sociological Review, 141 (1949),
221-235.

Bell, Howard H. "Chicago Negroes in the Reform Movement, 1847-1853," Negro History Bulletin, XXI
(April, 1958), 153-55.

_____ . "National Negro Conventions of the Middle
1840's: Moral Suasion vs. Political Actions,"
Journal of Negro History, XLII (October, 1957), 247-
260.

_____ . "The Negro Convention Movement, 1830-1860:
New Perspectives," Negro History Bulletin, XIV
(February 1951), 103-105, 114.

_____ . "The Negro National Council," Quarterly Review
of Higher Education Among Negroes, 28 (October,
1960), 258-264.

"The Birmingham Manifesto," Freedomways, 4, No. 1
(Winter, 1964).

Booker, Simeon. "Black Caucus," Ebony, XXVI, No. 11
(September, 1971), 100-105.

Brewer, James H. "The War Against Jim Crow in the Land
of Goshen," Negro History Bulletin, XXIV (December, 1960), 53-57.

Brooks, Maxwell R. "The March on Washington in Retrospect," Journal of Human Relations, XII (Fall, 1964), 73-87.

Brown, Lorenzo J. "The Sit-In Demonstration," Quarterly Review of Higher Education Among Negroes, XXIX (October, 1961), 293-296.

Bunche, Ralph J. "A Critical Analysis of the Tactics and Programs of Minority Groups," Journal of Negro Education, IV (July, 1935), 308-320.

_____. "The Program of Organizations Devoted to the Improvement of the Status of the American Negro," Journal of Negro Education, VIII (July 1, 1939), 539-550.

"Chicago Negro Labor and Civil Rights," Freedomways, 6, No. 4 (Fall, 1966).

Clark, Jacquelyne. "Standard Operational Procedures in Tragic Situations," Phylon, XXII (Winter, 1901), 318-328.

Clark, Kenneth B. "The Civil Rights Movement: Momentums and Organization," Daedalus, XCVI (Winter, 1966), 239-267.

Cox, Oliver C. "The Programs of Negro Civil Rights Organizations," Journal of Negro Education, XX (Summer, 1951), 354-366.

Dalfiume, Richard M. "The Forgotten Years of the Negro Revolution," Journal of American History, LV (June, 1968).

Davis, Lester. "The NAACP: A Leadership Dilemma," Freedomways, 1, No. 3 (Fall, 1961).

"Gloria Richardson: Lady General in Civil Rights," Ebony, XIX, No. 9 (July, 1964), 23.

God Healed Lady of the Crisis Bureau," Ebony, XXIII, No. 8 (June, 1968).

Gore, Robert B. "James Farmer of CORE," Negro History Bulletin, XXVIII (April, 1964), 160.

Granger, Lester B. "The National Negro Congress--An

Interpretation," Opportunity, XIV (May, 1936), 151-152.

_____. "The Negro Congress--Its Future," Opportunity, XVIII (June, 1940), 164-166.

Gross, Bella. "The First National Negro Convention," Journal of Negro History, XXXI (October, 1946), 435-443.

_____. "The Roots of the National Negro Convention," Negro History Bulletin, X (November, 1946), 40.

Gross, James A. "The NAACP at the AFL-CIO: An Overview," Negro History Bulletin, XXVI (November, 1964), 1.

Hamilton, J. Bims. "CORE: Wild Child of Civil Rights," Ebony, XX, No. 12 (October, 1965), 35-43.

Hatchett, John F. "The Negro Revolution: A Quest for Justice?" Journal of Human Relations, XIV (Spring, 1966), 406-420.

Johnson, Oakley C. "Negro Protest Thought in the Twentieth Century," Freedomways, 7, No. 1 (Winter, 1967).

Jones, Eugene K. "The National Urban League," Opportunity, III (January, 1925), 12-15.

Lewis, Roscoe E. "The Role of Pressure Groups in Maintaining Morale Among Negroes," Journal of Negro Education, XII (Summer, 1943), 464-473.

Lipsky, Roma. "Electioneering Among the Minorities," Commentary (May, 1961), 428-432.

McKibben, Davidson Burns. "Negro Slave Insurrections in Mississippi, 1800-1865," Journal of Negro History, XXIV No. 1 (January, 1949).

McPherson, James M. "Abolitionists and the Civil Rights Act of 1875," Journal of American History, LV (June, 1968).

"March on Washington," Freedomways, 2, No. 4 (Fall, 1963).

Meier, August. "Negro Protest Movements and Organizations," Journal of Negro Education, XXXII (Fall,
   1963), 437-450.

_____. "On the Role of Martin Luther King," New
   Politics, IV (Winter, 1965), 52-59.

_____, and Rudwick, Elliott. "The Boycott Movement
   against Jim Crow Street Cars in the South, 1900-
   1906," Journal of American History, XL (March,
   1969).

Miles, Edwin A. "The Mississippi Slave Insurrection Scare
   of 1835," Journal of Negro History, XXII, No. 4
   (October, 1959).

"NAACP's New Leader: Roy Wilkins Is Named Executive
   Secretary," Ebony, X, No. 7 (July, 1955), 17-23.

"National Urban League," Journal of Human Relations, VII
   (Autumn, 1958), 63-66.

"National Association for the Advancement of Colored People." Journal of Human Relations, VII (Autumn, 1958).

"N.E.A. Elects Negro Vice President," Negro History Bulletin, XVIII (October, 1964), 21.

"The New Freedom of the Independence Movement," Negro
   History Bulletin, I (December, 1937), 2-3.

Osofsky, Gilbert. "Race Riot, 1900: A Study of Ethnic
   Violence," Journal of Negro Education, XXXXII
   (Winter, 1963), 16-24.

Ovington, M. W. "The National Association for the Advancement of Colored People," Journal of Negro History, IX, No. 2 (April, 1924).

Petrof, John V. "The Effect of Student Boycotts upon the
   Purchasing Habits of Negro Families in Atlanta,
   Georgia," Negro Educational Review, VII (April,
   1956), 52-59.

Pinckney, Elrich. "The Sit-In Demonstrations, February
   23-28, 1960," Quarterly Review of Higher Education
   Among Negroes, XXIX (October, 1961), 271-273.

"Platform of the Niagara Movement," Outlook, 84 (Septem-
    ber 1, 1906), 3-4.

"Prayer Pilgrimage to Washington," Ebony, XII, No. 10
    (August 1956), 16.

"Profile of the NAACP," Negro History Bulletin, XXVII
    (January, 1964).

Record, Wilson. "The NAACP Versus Negro Revolutionary
    Protest," American Sociological Review, 21 (1956).

_____. "The Sociological Study of Action Organizations,"
    Journal of Human Relations, VII (Spring, 1959), 451-
    472.

Rich, Marvin. "The Congress of Racial Equality and Its
    Strategy," in Harry R. Mahood (ed.), Pressure
    Groups in American Politics (New York: Scribner,
    1967), 197-204.

Rose, Arnold N. "The Negroes Morale Group Identification
    and Protest," American Journal of Sociology, LVI
    (July, 1950-May, 1951).

Rowland, Stanley, Jr. "Legal War on the NAACP," The
    Nation, 184 (February 9, 1957), 115-116.

Royster, John W. "The Sit-Ins February," Quarterly Re-
    view of Higher Education Among Negroes, XXIX
    (October, 1961), 267-70.

Rudwick, Elliot M. "The Niagara Movement," Journal of
    Negro History, XLII (July, 1957), 177-200.

Sindler, A. P. "Negroes, Ethnic Groups and American
    Politics," Current History, 55 (October, 1968), 207-
    212.

Stampp, Kenneth M. "The Fate of the Southern Anti-Slavery
    Movement," Journal of Negro History, XXVIII (Janu-
    ary, 1943), 10-22.

"Student Non-Violent Coordinating Committee," Negro History
    Bulletin, XXVII (December, 1963), 50.

"Sustaining the Urban League," Opportunity (January, 1925),
    12-15.

Thompson, Daniel C. "Civil Rights Leadership: An Opinion Study," Journal of Negro Education, XXXII (Fall, 1963), 426-436.

_____. "The Rise of the Negro Protest," Journal of Human Relations, XIV (Fall, 1966), 56-73.

Thornbrough, Emma Lou. "The National Afro-American League, 1887-1908." Journal of Southern History, XXVII (November, 1961), 494-512.

Vose, Clement E. "Litigation as a Form of Pressure Group Activity," The Annals, 319 (September, 1958), 20-31.

Walton, Hanes, Jr. "The Political Leadership of Martin Luther King, Jr.," Quarterly Review of Higher Education Among Negroes, XXXVI (July, 1968), 163-171.

_____. "The Politics of Negro Educational Associations," Negro Educational Review, XX (January, 1969), 34-41.

Ware, Gilbert. "Lobbying as a Means of Protest: The NAACP as an Agent of Equality," Journal of Negro Education, XXXIII (Spring, 1964), 103-110.

Watson, Richard L., Jr. "The Defeat of Judge Parker: A Case Study in Pressure Groups and Politics," Mississippi Valley Historical Review, L (September, 1963), 213-234.

Wesley, Charles H. "The Negroes of New York in the Emancipation Movement," Journal of Negro History, XXIV (January, 1939), 65-103.

Williamson, James F. "A Study in 'Sit-In' Demonstrations as Reported in the Tampa Tribune, February-June, 1960," Quarterly Review of Higher Education Among Negroes, XXIX (October, 1961), 260-266.

Zangrando, Robert L. "The Direction of the March," Negro History Bulletin, XXVII (January, 1964), 74.

_____. "The NAACP and a Federal Anti-Lynching Bill, 1934-1940," Journal of Negro History, L (April, 1965).

Books

Barton, Rebecca Chalmers. Our Human Rights: A Study
in the Art of Persuasion. Washington, D.C.:
Public Affairs Press, 1955.

Bell, Inge. CORE And the Strategy of Non-Violence. New
York: Oxford University Press, 1963.

Burns, W. Haywood. The Voices of Negro Protest in America. New York: Oxford University Press, 1963.

Clark, Jacquelyne. These Rights They Seek: A Comparison
of Goals and Techniques of Local Civil Rights Organizations. Washington, D.C.: Public Affairs
Press, 1962.

Garfinkel, Herbert. When Negroes March: The March on
Washington Movement in the Organizational Politics
for F.E.P.C. Glencoe: Free Press, 1959.

Hughes, Langston. Fight for Freedom: The Story of the
National Association for the Advancement of Colored
People. New York: W. W. Norton, 1963.

Jack, Robert L. History of the National Association for the
Advancement of Colored People. Boston: Meador
Publishing Company, 1943.

Kellogg, Charles F. NAACP: A History of the National
Association for the Advancement of Colored People.
(Vol. 1, 1909-1920. Baltimore: Johns Hopkins
Press, 1967.

King, Donald B. and Quick, Charles W. (ed.) Legal Aspects
of the Civil Rights Movement. Detroit: Wayne
State University Press, 1965.

Peck, James. Freedom Ride. New York: Simon and
Schuster, 1962.

Saddler, Gordon T. The NAACP: The Struggle in the Fulfillment of American Idealism. The Welch Publishing Company, 1956.

St. James, Warren D. The National Association for the
Advancement of Colored People: A Case Study in

Pressure Groups. New York: Exposition Press, 1958.

Sindler, Allan P. Negro Protest and Local Politics in Durham, North Carolina. New York: McGraw-Hill, 1965.

Strickland, Arvarh E. History of the Chicago Urban League. Urbana: University of Illinois Press, 1966.

They Shall Overcome: CORE Report to the America Conscience. New York: W. W. Norton Company, 1965.

Zinn, Howard. SNCC: The New Abolitionists. Boston: Beacon Press, 1964.

Dissertations

Bell, Howard. A Survey of the Negro Convention Movement 1830-1861. Northwestern University, 1953.

Clark, Jacquelyne M. J. Goals and Techniques in Three Negro Civil Rights Organizations in Alabama. Ohio State University, 1960.

Gross, James A. The NAACP, the AFL-CIO and the Negro Worker. University of Wisconsin, 1962.

Hazel, David W. The National Association for the Advancement of Colored People and the National Legislative Process. University of Michigan, 1957.

Lewis, Edward S. The Urban League, a Dynamic Instrument in Social Change: A Study of the Changing Role of the New York Urban League, 1910-1960. New York University, 1961.

Oppenheimer, Martin. The Genesis of the Southern Negro Student Movement (Sit-in Movement): A Study in Contemporary Negro Protest. University of Pennsylvania, 1963.

Ware, Gilbert. The National Association for the Advancement of Colored People and the Civil Rights Act of 1957. Princeton University, 1962.

White, Robert M.   The Tallahassee Sit-ins and CORE: A
     Non-Violent Revolutionary Submovement.   Florida
     State University, 1964.

Zangrando, Robert L.   The Efforts of the NAACP to Secure
     Passage of a Federal Anti-Lynching Law.   University
     of Pennsylvania, 1963.

Chapter VI

BLACK POLITICAL CANDIDATES

The popular Georgia state assemblyman, Julian Bond, published a pamphlet in 1969 on Black Southern Campaign Experiences. It was the first study of its kind in the field of black politics.

In this volume Bond interviewed several black candidates, both successful and unsuccessful ones, and tried to get a picture of their activities ranging from campaign speeches to finances, platforms, sources of support and the nature of their electoral responses. With more than 1, 500 black elected officials in the political arena, this type of analysis was sorely needed. But Bond's study lacked vigor, methodology, a systematic approach; like the numerous other essays that would soon arrive on the scene, it was journalistic, impressionistic, sketchy.

Most of the literature in this area is merely descriptive, colorful and laudatory, not really analytical, comprehensive and structural. The majority of the essays have been done by reporters, free-lance writers, and politicians themselves. Little in this area has been prepared by scholars and trained specialists.

An essay by Professor Leslie McLemore and Hanes Walton, Jr., entitled "Portrait of Black Political Styles," was an attempt to develop a typology of the styles of black political candidates. While the essay tried to create four discernible categories of black political styles, much more is needed in view of the increasing number of blacks who are entering the political arena on all levels.

In the future, books on black mayors, aldermen, congressional, gubernatorial and presidential candidates and others can be expected in greater numbers, and they are sorely needed, both by the layman and the specialist alike. The work by Alex Poinsett, Black Power Gray Style, which deals with the making of black mayors in a major urban city, is ground-breaking and offers leads for the future.

MEN, MOTIVATION AND EXPECTATIONS

Articles

"Adam Clayton Powell and the Politics of Race," Freedom-ways, 6, No. 2 (Spring, 1966).

"A Politician Who Kept His Promise," Ebony, XII, No. 1, (November, 1956).

"Wright, Chester M. "Reflections of a Losing Candidate," The Black Politician.

"Young Politician with a Conscience," Ebony, XVII, No. 4 (February, 1962), 111-113.

AUTOBIOGRAPHIES--BIOGRAPHIES

Articles

Feldman, E. "James T. Rapier, 1839-1884," Negro History Bulletin, 20 (December, 1956), 62-66.

Llorens, David. "Julian Bond," Ebony, XXII, No. 7 (May, 1969), 58-70.

Dissertations

Abbott, Richard H. Cobbler in Congress: Life of Henry Wilson, 1812-1875. University of Wisconsin, 1965.

St. Claire, Saide D. The National Career of Blanche Kelso
    Bruce. New York University, 1947.

Books

Adams, Russell L. Great Negroes, Past and Present.
    Chicago: Afro-Am, 1963.

Bardolph, Richard. The Negro Vanguard. New York:
    Rinehart, 1959.

Bennett, Lerone Jr. What Manner of Man: A Biography of
    Martin Luther King. Chicago: Johnson, 1964.

Bond, Mildred. Negro Heroes of Emancipation. New York:
    NAACP, 1964.

Chestnutt, Charles Waddell. Frederick Douglass. Boston:
    Small, Maynard and Company, 1899.

Feldman, Eugene Pieter Romayn. Black Power in Old
    Alabama: The Life and Stirring Times of James T.
    Rapier, Afro-American Congressman from Alabama,
    1839-1883. Chicago: Museum of African-American
    History, 1968.

Garvey, Amy Jacques. Garvey and Garveyism. Kingston,
    Jamaica: Published by the author, 1963. (Available
    from University Place Bookshop, 840 Broadway, New
    York, N.Y. 10003).

Kugelmass, J. Alvin. Ralph J. Bunche, Fighter for Peace.
    New York: Messner, 1952.

Lawson, Elizabeth. The Gentleman from Mississippi. New
    York. Published by the author. N.D. (Pamphlet)

Metcalf, George R. Black Profiles. New York: McGraw-
    Hill, 1968.

BLACK PRESIDENTIAL CANDIDATES

Articles

Greeley, A. M. "For a Black Vice President in 1972,"
New York Times Magazine (September 19, 1971), 28.

Romaine, H. "Why a Black Man Should Run," Nation, 213
(September 27, 1971), 264-268.

Wieck, P. R. "On the Chisholm Campaign Trail," New
Republic. 165 (December 4, 1971), 16-18.

BLACK GUBERNATORIAL CANDIDATES

Articles

O'Neal, Paul. "A Black Governor for Mississippi," Life,
79, No. 10 (May 14, 1971), 56-60.

"Virgin Islands Governor," Ebony, XII, No. 2 (December,
1956), 119.

BLACK CONGRESSIONAL CANDIDATES

Articles

Becker, John F. and Eugene E. Heaton, Jr. "Election of
Senator Edward W. Brooke," Public Opinion Quarterly, 31 (Fall, 1967), 346-358.

Bennett, Lerone, Jr. "Adam Clayton Powell, Enigma on
Capitol Hill," Ebony, 18 (June, 1963), 25-28.

"Black Caucus in Congress: How It Is Faring," U.S. News
& World Report, 72 (February 14, 1972), 86-87.

Booker, Simeon. "Adam Clayton Powell: Man Behind the
Controversy," Ebony, XXII, No. 5 (March, 1967),
27-34.

_____. "A New Face in Congress--John Conyers, Jr.
Is Sixth Negro U.S. Representative," Ebony, XX, No.
3 (January, 1951), 75-78.

Bowle, S. J. "Southern Representation in Congress,"
     Independent, 60 (January 18, 1906), 151-154.

"Capital Welcomes 4th Negro Congressman," Ebony, XII,
     No. 11 (September, 1958), 98-102.

Chambers, A. A. "Negro in Congress of the United States,"
     Negro History Bulletin, 24 (March, 1961), 143.

Cheek, William F. "A Negro Runs for Congress: John
     Mercer Langston and the Virginia Campaign of 1888,"
     Journal of Negro History, 52 (January, 1967), 14-34.

"Congressman from Mississippi," Freedomways, 5, No. 2
     (Spring, 1965).

"Congressman Mitchell's Speech on Negro History in the
     United States House of Representatives, February 7,
     1949," Negro History Bulletin, 111 (March, 1940),
     85.

"Congresswoman Shirley Chisholm," Vogue, 153 (May, 1969),
     58-59.

"First Black Woman in the U.S. House of Representatives,"
     Negro History Bulletin, XXXIII (May, 1970), 128.

"First Black Woman on Capitol Hill," Ebony, 24 (February,
     1969), 58-59.

"First Negro in Congress," Senior Scholastic, 87 (Decem-
     ber 9, 1965), 7.

Gruenberg, R. "Dawson of Illinois," Nation, 183 (Septem-
     ber 8, 1956), 196-198.

Houston, David G. "A Negro Senator," Journal of Negro
     History, VII, No. 3 (July, 1922).

Jarret, Calvin. "The First Negro Senator," Negro Digest,
     XIII (May, 1964).

Katz, W. "George Henry White: A Militant Negro Con-
     gressman in the Age of Booker T. Washington,"
     Negro History Bulletin, 29 (March, 1966), 125-126.

Massoquori, Hans J. " 'Gus' Hawkins--Fifth Negro

Congressman, " Ebony, XVIII (February, 1963), 38-
42.

Menard, E.   "John Willis Menard: First Negro Elected to
the U. S. Congress, " Negro History Bulletin, 28
(December, 1964), 53-54.

Miller, Judy Ann.   "The Representative Is a Lady, " The
Black Politician, I (Fall, 1969), 17-18.

"Mr. Diggs Goes to Congress, " Ebony, X, No. 7 (April,
1955), 104-108.

Morrison, Allan.   "Adam Clayton Powell Returns to Harlem, " Ebony, XX, No. 9 (July, 1965), 80-88.

"Negro Candidates for Congress, " New Republic, 122 (June
12, 1950), 7-8.

"Negro Congressman C. Diggs, Jr. , " Negro History Bulletin, 27 (February, 1964), 114.

"Negro Congressmen of the Reconstruction Era, " Negro History Bulletin, XXII (January, 1959), 74, 95.

"Negro Senators from Mississippi, " Ebony, XI, No. 7 (May,
1956), 65-66, 70.

"Negroes in Congress, 1868-1895, " Negro History Bulletin,
XXXI (November, 1968), 12-13.

"New Faces in Congress, " Ebony, XXIV (February, 1969),
56-65.

O'Hare, Lee.   "The Senator from Massachusetts, " Political
Affairs, 46 (January, 1967), 15-23.

Rabb, C.   "Black Freshmen: Clay, Chisholm and Stokes, "
Nation, 208 (January 6, 1969), 6-7.

"Reduction of Southern Representation in Congress, " Outlook,
79 (January 7, 1905), 11-15.

Roy, Jessie.   "Early Negro Congressmen, " Negro History
Bulletin XIV (December, 1950), 59.

Sheehan, E. R. F.   "Brooke of Massachusetts;   A Negro

Governor on Beacon Hill?" Harper's Magazine, 228 (June, 1964), 41-47.

Slaff, G. "Five Seats in Congress; Mississippi Challenge," Nation, 200 (May 17, 1965), 526-528.

Taylor, Alrutheus A. "Negro Congressmen a Generation After," Journal of Negro History, VII (April, 1922), 127-171.

"Three Negro Senators of the United States," Negro History Bulletin, 30 (January, 1967), 4-5+.

Urofsky, Melvin I. "Blanche K. Bruce: United States Senator, 1875-1881," Journal of Mississippi History, 29 (May, 1967), 118-141.

Walton, L. A. "Negro Comes Back to the United States Congress," Current History, 30 (June, 1929), 461-463.

Walton, N. W. "James T. Rapier: Congressman from Alabama," Negro History Bulletin, 30 (November, 1967), 6-10.

"Will California Send a Negro to the Senate?" Ebony, XIX, No. 3 (January, 1964), 25.

Wilson, James. "The Flamboyant Mr. Powell," Commentary (January 1966), 31-35.

Wilson, James Q. "Two Negro Politicians: An Interpretation," Midwest Journal of Political Science, 4 (November, 1960), 346-369.

Woodward, Maurice C. "The Legislative Record of Adam Clayton Powell Revisited," The Black Politician (July, 1971).

Work, Monroe N., (comp.) "Some Negro Members of Reconstruction Conventions and Legislatures of Congress," Journal of Negro History, V (January, 1928), 63-125.

Books

Hamilton, James. Negro Suffrage and Congressional Repre-
    sentation. New York: Winthrop Press, 1910.

Hickey, Neil and Edwin Ed. Adam Clayton Powell and the
    Politics of Race. New York: Fleet Publishing Cor-
    poration, 1965.

Magdel, Edward. Owen Lovejoy: Abolitionist in Congress.
    New Brunswick, New Jersey: Rutgers University
    Press, 1967.

Moseley, J. H. Sixty Years in Congress and Twenty-Eight
    Out. New York: Vantage Press, 1960.

Smith, Samuel D. The Negro in Congress, 1870-1901.
    New York: Kennikat Press, 1966.

BLACK STATE AND LOCAL CANDIDATES

Articles

Bacote, Clarence A. "Negro Officeholders in Georgia under
    President McKinley," Journal of Negro History,
    XLIV (July, 1959), 195-216.

_____. "William Lynch, Negro Councilman, and Political
    Activities in Atlanta During Early Reconstruction,"
    Journal of Negro History, XL, No. 4 (October, 1955).

Bennett, Lerone. "Georgia's Negro Senator," Ebony, XVIII,
    No. 5 (March, 1963), 25-34.

"Black Day in Eutaw; Negro Election Triumph in Greene
    County, Alabama," Newsweek, 74 (August 11, 1969),
    24-25.

"Black Elected Officials in the United States," Negro History
    Bulletin, XXXIII (November, 1970), 168.

Bolden, Richard. "The Role of the Negro Legislature in
    Georgia." Unpublished M.A. Thesis, Atlanta Uni-
    versity, 1969.

Boulware, M. H. "Roscoe Conkling Simmons: The Golden

Voiced Politico," Negro History Bulletin, 29 (March, 1966), 131-132.

Brittain, J. M. "Return of the Negro to Alabama Politics, 1930-1954," Negro History Bulletin, 22 (May, 1959), 196-199.

Brown, Arthur Z. "Participation of Negroes in the Reconstruction Legislatures of Texas," Negro History Bulletin, XX (January, 1957), 87-88.

Brown, Charles A. "A. H. Curtis: An Alabama Legislator 1870-1876," Negro History Bulletin, 25 (February, 1962), 79-101.

_____. "John Dozier: A Member of the General Assembly of Alabama 1872-1873 and 1873-1874," Negro History Bulletin, 26 (December, 1962), 113.

_____. "Reconstruction Legislators in Alabama," Negro History Bulletin (March, 1963), 198-200.

_____. "William Hooper Council, Alabama Legislature, Editor and Lawyer," Negro History Bulletin, XXVI (February 1963), 171.

"Coolidge on Colored Candidates," Literary Digest, 82 (August 30, 1924), 13.

Coulter, E. Merton. "Aaron Alpeonia Bradley, Georgia Negro Politician During Reconstruction Times," Georgia Historical Quarterly, 51 (March, 1967), 15-41; (June, 1967), 154-174; (September, 1967), 264-306.

_____. "Tunis G. Campbell, Negro Reconstructionist in Georgia," Georgia Historical Quarterly, 51 (December, 1967), 401-424; (March, 1968), 16-52.

Fleming, G. James. "An All-Negro Ticket in Baltimore," Eagleton Institute, New York: McGraw-Hill, 1963.

"Georgia Legislature's New Look for 1966--'One Man, One Vote' Ruling Yields 10 Seats for Negroes," Ebony, XX, No. 11 (September, 1965), 48-55.

Gosnell, Harold F. and R. E. Martin, "The Negro as

Voter and Officeholder," Journal of Negro Education, XXXII (Fall, 1963), 415-425.

"Governor's Right Hand Man," Ebony, XV, No. 11 (September, 1960), 75-80.

Jewell, Malcolm. "State Legislatures in Southern Politics," Journal of Politics, XXVI (February, 1964), 177-196.

Johnson, James Hugo. "The Participation of Negroes in the Government in Virginia from 1877-1888," Journal of Negro History, XIV, No. 3 (July, 1929).

Jones, Mack H. "Black Officeholders in Local Governments of the South: An Overview," Politics 71.

McCree, Wade H., Jr. "The Negro Renaissance in Michigan Politics," Negro History Bulletin, XXVI (October, 1962), 7-13.

"Milwaukee's First Lady Councilman," Ebony, XIII, No. 8 (June, 1968), 40-44.

"Nation's Youngest Lawmaker," Ebony, 19 (June, 1964), 135.

"Negro Politician Succeeds in Texas," Ebony, XVI, No. 11 (September, 1961), 23-30.

"Negro Runs for State Office in Boston," Look, 24 (November 8, 1960), 111-112+.

"The Negro Woman in Politics," Ebony, XXI, No. 10 (August, 1966).

"One Black Plum: Result of Negroes' Election Drive in Alabama," Newsweek, 67 (June 13, 1966), 44.

"Other Half of the Battle: Southern Black Officeholders," Time, 93 (January 10, 1969), 22.

"Practical Politician: Julian Bond," The Black Politician, I (Fall, 1969), 28-30.

Roberts, G. "Remarkable Thing Is Happening in Wilcox County, Alabama; Negro Candidate for Sheriff," New York Times Magazine (April 17, 1966), 26-28.

Rose, Harold. "The All Negro Town: Its Evolution and Future," Geographical Review, LXV (July, 1965), 362-381.

"Second Reconstruction, Alabama Negroes File for Office Around the State," Newsweek, 67 (March 21, 1966), 28-29.

Shapiro, Herbert. "Julian Bond: Georgia's 'Uppity' Legislator," The Nation, 202 (February 7, 1966), 145-148.

Sisk, Glenn. "The Negro in Atlanta Politics," Negro History Bulletin, XXVII (October, 1964), 17.

"Southern Delegate Scandal," Literary Digest, 80 (January 5, 1924), 472-473.

"States Boast Record Number of Negro Lawmakers," Ebony, XX, No. 6 (April, 1965), 191-197.

Streaten, A. "Politics of Self-Determination: Harlem's Negro City Councilman," Commonweal, 42 (August 17, 1945), 425-427.

"Things to Come; Negroes in the Georgia House of Representatives," New Republic, 152 (May 3, 1965), 7.

"Town Moderator," Ebony, VIII (October, 1953), 53-58.

Wells, Janet. "43 Blacks Win Elections in Three Southern States," VEP News (May, 1969), 1-10.

White, James B. "Changing Interpretations of the Negro in the Reconstruction Governments," Negro History Bulletin, XXII (November, 1958), 31-34.

"Women in Politics," Ebony, XI, No. 10 (August, 1956).

Books

Bond, Julian. Black Candidates: Southern Campaign Experiences. Atlanta: Southern Regional Council, 1969.

Brewer, J. Mason. Negro Legislators of Texas. Dallas: Mathis Publishing Company, 1935.

Bryant, Lawrence C. (ed.) Negro Legislators in South
    Carolina, 1865-1894: Preliminary Report. Orange-
    burg, South Carolina: School of Graduate Studies,
    South Carolina State College, 1966.

Clayton, Edward T. The Negro Politician: His Success
    and Failures. Chicago: Johnson Publishing Company,
    1964.

Coulter, E. Merton. Negro Legislators in Georgia During
    the Reconstruction Period. Athens: Georgia His-
    torical Quarterly, 1968.

Davis, Benjamin T. Communist Councilman from Harlem.
    New York: International Publishers, 1969.

Fleming, G. James. An All-Negro Ticket in Baltimore.
    New York: Holt, 1960.

Jackson, Luther P. Negro Officeholders in Virginia, 1865-
    1895. Norfolk, Virginia: Guide Quality Press, 1945.

Morris, John B., ed. Black Elected Officials in the
    Southern States. Atlanta: Southern Regional Council,
    1969.

National Roster of Black Elected Officials. Washington,
    D.C.: Metropolitan Applied Research Center, 1970.

Watters, Pat and Reese Cleghorn. Climbing Jacob's Ladder:
    The Arrival of Negroes in Southern Politics. New
    York: Harcourt, Brace and World, 1967.

BLACK MAYORS

Articles

"The Black Mayors," Ebony, XXV (February, 1970), 76-84.

"Black Mayors Discuss State of the Nation," Ebony, XXV,
    No. 4 (February, 1970), 76-78, 80-84.

"Black Mayors in Florida Town," Ebony, XXVI, No. 10
    (August 1971), 82-85.

Booker, Simeon. "Can Negroes Become Big City Mayors?"

Ebony, XXI, No. 5 (March, 1966), 22.

"Breakthrough in Chapel Hill," Time, 93 (May 16, 1969), 26.

"Changing Times; R. Henry Sworn in as Mayor of Spring-
       field, Ohio," Newsweek, 67 (January 17, 1966), 27.

Daley, Mary Dowling. "Mayor Stokes' West Side Story,"
       Commenweal, 91 (November 28, 1969), 270-271.

"First Mayor of the Nation's Capitol," Negro History Bul-
       letin, 30 (November, 1967), 3-5.

"First Negro Mayor of Cleveland, Ohio," Negro History
       Bulletin, 31 (March, 1968), 4.

Fleming, G. James. "Baltimore's Failure to Elect a Black
       Mayor in 1972," Joint Center for Political Studies,
       1972.

Hadden, Jeffrey K., et al. "Making of the Negro Mayors,
       1967," Transaction, 6 (January, 1968), 21-30.

Lantz, Ragni. "D.C. 'Mayor' Walter Washington," Ebony,
       XXIII, No. 5 (March, 1968), 72-77.

"Mayor of Chapel Hill," Newsweek, 73 (May 19, 1969), 41.

"Michigan's Negro Mayors," Ebony, XXII, No. 9 (July,
       1967), 74-82.

Naughton, James. "Mayor Stokes: The First Hundred Days,"
       New York Times Magazine (February, 1968), 26-27,
       48-62.

_____, and Berkeley Rice. "In Cleveland and Boston:
       The Issue Is Race," The New York Times Magazine
       (November, 1967), 30-32, 97-130.

"Not Doing You Like You Done Us; First Black Mayor of
       a Racially Mixed Mississippi Town Since Reconstruc-
       tion," Time, 94 (July 18, 1969), 16.

Stokes, Carl B. and Richard G. Hatcher. "My First Year
       in Office," Ebony, XXIV, No. 3 (January, 1969), 116-
       122.

"The Vice Mayor of Richmond," Ebony, XXII, No. 1 (November, 1966), 176-178.

"Vote Power; Gary's Negroes Nominate R. Hatcher as Democratic Mayoral Candidate," Time, 86 (May 12, 1967), 21-22.

Books

Nelson, William E., Jr. Electing Black Mayors: Political Action in the Black Community. Charles Merrill. (Forthcoming.)

Weinberg, Kenneth C. Black Victory: Carl Stokes and the Winning of Cleveland. Chicago: Quadrangle, 1968.

BLACK CABINET MEMBERS

Articles

Booker, Simeon. "Black Man in the White House," Ebony, XVI, No. 6 (April, 1961), 71-86.

Cartwright, Marguerite. "Ralph J. Bunche United Nations Mediator," Negro History Bulletin, XIX (May, 1956), 174.

"Let's Give Him a Chance; Negroes in the Nixon Administration," Ebony, 24 (April, 1969), 52-53.

"Military Aide to LBJ: H. Robinson," Ebony, 22 (November, 1966), 96-98.

"Nixon Makes Two Black Appointees: E. D. Koontz and J. Farmer," Negro History Bulletin, 32 (April, 1969), 20-21.

Sanders, Charles L. "Ambassador Is a Lady," Ebony, XXI, No. 3 (January, 1966), 200.

"White House Administration," Ebony, XII, No. 7 (May, 1957), 60-63.

"White House Press Aide," Ebony, XVI, No. 5 (March, 1961), 91-92.

BLACK POLITICAL CAMPAIGNS

Articles

Black, E.   "Southern Governors and Political Change:
     Campaign Stances on Racial Segregation and Econom-
     ic Development, 1950-69," Journal of Politics, 233
     (August, 1971), 590-621.

Boyd, James.   "Strategy for Negroes," The Nation, 156
     (June 26, 1943), 884-887.

Dowd, D. F.   "The Campaign in Fayette County," Monthly
     Review (April, 1964), 675-679.

Herron, Jeannine.   "Mississippi's Underground Election:
     Negro Mock Campaign," The Nation, 197 (December
     7, 1963), 387-389.

"In Search of a Black Strategy," Time, 98 (December 20,
     1971), 9-10.

Poinsett, A.   "Black Political Strategies for '72," Ebony,
     27 (February, 1972), 66-69.

"Political Rally," Freedomways, 6, No. 4 (1966).

Waugh, John C.   "Tom Bradley's Non-Partisan, Bi-partisan
     Coalition Campaign," The Black Politician, I
     (Fall, 1969), 9-11.

Chapter VII

BLACK POLITICAL BEHAVIOR

Among the least studied areas of black politics are
the behavioral aspects. Voting studies abound but the psychological, sociological, mathematical, and methodological
formulations are still few in number. A principal reason
has been the lack of relevant data on the past aspects and
features of blacks in political life. Until a significant
amount of such data has been assembled, the behavioral
studies have little basis to rest on. Secondly, the money
needed to carry out survey analyses, interviewing, polling,
and in-depth psychological studies has not been available.

Black political behavior received its first major impact when Donald Matthews and James Prothro released their
work on Negroes and the New Southern Politics. The work,
unfortunately, stops at 1966, before the 1965 Voting Rights
Act had its full impact and the number of blacks elected officials increased dramatically.

Articles

Abrahams, Samuel. "Negro Disfranchisement," Negro
   History Bulletin, XII (February, 1949), 103-105, 119.

Adams, J. T. "Disfranchisement of Negroes in New
   England," American Historical Review (April, 1925),
   543-547.

Adelman, B. "Birth of a Voter: Louisiana Parish Registers
   1st Negro in Sixty-One Years," Ebony, 19 (February,

1964), 88-90.

"Alabama's New Era: The Negro Votes," Newsweek, 67 (May 16, 1966), 25-30.

Alexander, Herbert B. "The Political Progress of the Negro," Negro History Bulletin, IV (May, 1941), 185.

Allswang, John. "The Chicago Negro Voters and the Democratic Consensus: A Case Study, 1918-1936," in B. Sternsher, (ed.), The Negro in Depression and War (Chicago: Quadrangle Books, 1969), 234-257.

Andrews, Norman P. "The Negro in Politics," Journal of Negro History, V (October, 1920), 420-436.

"Attacking Segregation," Negro History Bulletin, IX (June, 1946), 194, 215.

Bacote, Clarence A. "The Negro in Atlanta Politics," Phylon, XVI (Winter, 1955), 333-350.

_____. "The Negro Voter in Georgia Politics Today," Journal of Negro Education, XXVI (Summer, 1957), 307-318.

_____. "Some Aspects of Negro Life in Georgia, 1880-1908," Journal of Negro History, XLIII (July, 1958), 186-213.

Baker, Ray Stannard. "Negro in Politics," American Magazine, 66 (June, 1908), 169-180.

_____. "Negro Suffrage in a Democracy," Atlantic Monthly, CVI (November, 1910), 612-619.

Bashful, Emmet W. "Registration and Voting Among Members of the Florida State Teachers Association," Negro History Bulletin (December, 1956).

"The Battle for the Ballot," The Nation, 175 (September 27, 1952), 250-251.

Bennett, Lerone, Jr. "Black Power, Part II," Ebony, XXI, No. 6 (December, 1965).

Bernd, Joseph L. and Holland, Lynwood M. "Recent Restrictions upon Negro Suffrage: The Case of Georgia," Journal of Politics, 21 (August, 1959), 487-513.

Beth, L. P. "The White Primary and the Judicial Function in the United States," Political Quarterly, XXIX (October-December, 1958), 366-377.

Bickel, Alexander M. "Voting Rights Bill Is Tough," New Republic, CLII (April 3, 1965), 16-18.

"Black Balloting," Review of Reviews, 76 (December, 1929), 649-650.

"Black Politics Takes a Different Turn," U.S. News and World Report, 71 (September 20, 1971), 57-60.

Blackford, Staige. "The Twenty-Fourth Amendment," New South, XIX (February, 1964), 13-15.

Blaine, James G., et al. "Ought the Negro to be Disfranchised, Ought He to Have Been Enfranchised?" North American Review, CXXVIII (March, 1829), 226-228.

Booker, Simeon. "Baltimore Negro Vote Capitol," Ebony, XV, No. 2 (December, 1958).

Brewer, William M. "The Poll Tax and the Poll Taxers," Journal of Negro History (July, 1944).

Brisbane, R. H. "The Negro's Growing Political Power," The Nation, 175 (September 27, 1952), 248-249.

Brittain, Joseph M. "Some Reflections on Negro Suffrage in Alabama--Past and Present," Journal of Negro History, XLVII (April, 1962), 127-138.

Broder, David S. "Negro Vote Upset Off-Year Pattern," New York Times (November 4, 1965).

Bullock, Henry A. "Expansion of Negro Suffrage in Texas," Journal of Negro Education, XXVII (Summer, 1957), 377-396.

Bunche, Ralph J. "The Negro in the Political Life of the

United States," Journal of Negro Education, X (July, 1941), 567-584.

_____. "The Role of the University in the Political Orientation of Negro Youth," Journal of Negro Education, IX (October, 1940), 571-579.

_____. "The Thompson--Negro Alliance," Opportunity, VII (March, 1929), 78-80.

Caffey, Francis G. "Suffrage Limitations at the South," Political Science Quarterly, XX (1905), 53.

Carleton, William G. and Price, Hugh D. "America's Newest Voter: A Florida Case Study," Antioch Review, 14 (1954), 441-457.

Carter, Douglas. "Atlanta: Smart Politics and Good Race Relations," The Reporter, V (July 11, 1952), 18-21.

Chester, C. M. "Recollections of Reconstruction: Registering the Negro," Review of Reviews, 12 (October, 1895), 457-458.

Clark, E. P. "Ballot in Mississippi," Nation, 55 (August 25, 1892), 139-140.

_____. "Disfranchising a Race: Race Question in Mississippi," Nation, 66 (May 26, 1898), 398.

Clark, Kenneth B. "The Present Dilemma of the Negro," Journal of Negro History, LIII, No. 1 (January, 1968).

Clayton, Horace R. "The Negro's Challenge," The Nation, 157 (July 3, 1943), 10-12.

Cook, Samuel DuBois. "From Subject and Victim to Citizen and Public Official: An Historical Overview of the Negro in the Southern Political Process," Proceedings of Southwide Conference of Black Elected Officials. (Voter Education Project, Southern Regional Council, Atlanta, Georgia).

_____. "Political Movements and Organization," Journal of Politics, XXVII (February, 1964), 130-153.

_____. "The Tragic Myth of Black Power," New South
(Summer, 1966), 58-64.

Cothran, Tilman C. and Phillips, William M.   "Expansion
of Negro Suffrage in Arkansas," Journal of Negro
Education, XXVI (Summer, 1957), 287-296.

Cotton, R. and Hunt, H.   "Negro Politics Old Style and
New: Chicago and Mississippi," The Reporter, 35
(August 11, 1966), 21-23.

Daniel, Johnie.   "Changes in Negro Political Mobilization
and its Relationship to Community Socio-economic
Structure," Journal of Social and Behavioral Sciences,
XIII (Fall, 1968), 41-46.

DeGrazia, Alfred.   "A New Way Toward Equal Suffrage,"
New York University Law Review, 34 (1959), 716-
724.

"Deluge: Negro Registration in the South," Newsweek,
66 (August 23, 1965), 17-18.

Dent, Thomas C.   "Negro Politics," Freedomways, 6, No.
3 (Summer, 1966).

"Desegregation Resistance Slows Negro Registration,"
New South (October, 1959), 3-5.

"Disfranchisement in Alabama."   Outlook, 68 (May 4, 1901),
2.

"Disfranchisement of the Negro," Scribner's Magazine, 36
(July, 1904), 15-24.

Dorsey, Emmett E.   "The American Negro and His Government, 1961," Crisis, LXVIII (October, 1961), 467-
478.

Douglas, P. H.   "Trends and Developments: The 1960
Voting Rights Bill, The Struggle, The Final Results
and the Reason," Journal of Intergroup Relations, I
(Summer, 1960), 86-88.

DuBois, W. E. B.   "Negro Since 1900: A Progress Report," New York Times Magazine (November 21,
1948), 24+.

_____. "Progress Report on Negro America," Negro
        Digest, VII (May, 1949).

Duke, Paul. "Southern Politics and the Negroes,"
        Reporter, 31 (December 17, 1964), 18-21.

Dyer, Brainerd. "One Hundred Years of Negro Suffrage,"
        Pacific Historical Review, XXXVII (February, 1968).

Dykstra, Robert R. and Harlan Hahn. "Northern Voters
        and Negro Suffrage: The Case of Iowa, 1868," Pub-
        lic Opinion Quarterly, 32 (Summer, 1968), 202-215.

Farris, C. D. "The Re-enfranchisement of Negroes in
        Florida," Journal of Negro History, XLIV (October,
        1959), 259-283.

Fenton, John H. "The Negro Voter in Louisiana," Journal
        of Negro Education, XXVII (Summer, 1957), 319-328.

_____, and Vines, Kenneth N. "Negro Registration in
        Louisiana," American Political Science Review, LI
        (September, 1970).

Fishel, Leslie. "The Negro in Northern Politics 1870-
        1900," Mississippi Valley Historical Review, XLII
        (December, 1955), 466-489.

_____. "Northern Prejudice and Negro Suffrage 1865-
        1870," Journal of Negro History, XXIX (January,
        1954), 8-26.

_____. "Wisconsin and Negro Suffrage," Wisconsin
        Magazine of History, XLVI (Spring, 1963), 180-189.

Fleming, G. James. "The Negro in American Politics:
        The Past," in J. P. Davis, (ed.), The American
        Negro Reference Book (New Jersey: Prentice-Hall,
        1966), 414-430.

Forbes, G. W. "Progress of the Negro," Arena, 32
        (August, 1904), 134-141.

Foster, Vera C. "Beswellianism Techniques in the Restric-
        tion of Negro Voting," Phylon, X (Fall, 1949), 26-
        30.

Fox, Dixon. "The Negro Vote in Old New York," Political

Science Quarterly (June, 1917), 252-275.

"Franchise in the South," New Republic, 112 (January 15, 1945), 72.

Franklin, Bostic F.   "The Political Future of the Negro," Opportunity, XIV (June, 1936), 167-169.

Franklin, John Hope.   "Legal Disfranchisement of the Negro," Journal of Negro Education, XXVI (Summer, 1957), 241-248.

Galbraith, J. K.   "Negro Voting Power; Galbraith Explains its Force," U.S. News and World Report, 53 (September 10, 1962), 26.

Gamarekien, Edward.   "A Report from the South on the Negro Voter," The Reporter, XVI (June 27, 1957), 9-12.

Garland, Phyl.   "A Taste of Triumph for Black Mississippi," Ebony, XXIII, No. 4 (February, 1968), 25-32.

Gatlin, Douglas S.   "A Case Study of a Negro Voter's League: Political Studies Program Research Report No. 2."   University of North Carolina Department of Political Science, March, 1960.

Gaunlett, John and John B. McConaughy.   "Some Observations on the Influence of the Income Factor on Urban Negro Voting in South Carolina," Journal of Negro Education (Winter, 1962), 78-82.

_____. _____.   "Survey of Urban Negro Voting Behavior in South Carolina," South Carolina Law Quarterly (Spring, 1962), 365.

Gill, Robert L.   "Negro Citizens of Baltimore--Their Rights, Duties and Obligations," Morgan Bulletin (January, 1946).

Gomillion, C. G.   "The Negro Voter in Alabama," Journal of Negro Education XXVI (Summer, 1957), 281-286.

Gosnell, Harold F.   "Chicago Black Belt as a Political Battleground," American Journal of Sociology, 39 (November, 1933), 329-341.

_____. "The Negro Vote in Northern Cities," National
Municipal Review, XXX (May, 1961).

Grimes, Alan P. "Negro Suffrage and Nineteenth Century
Liberalism: Views of the New York Nation During
Reconstruction," Negro History Bulletin, XIV
(December, 1950), 55-57, 67-68.

Guyot, Lawrence and Mike Thelwell. "The Politics of
Necessity and Survival in Mississippi," Freedomways,
6, No. 2 (Spring, 1966).

_____. _____. "Toward Independent Politics Power,"
Freedomways, 6, No. 3 (Summer, 1966).

Hamilton, Charles V. "Black Americans and the Modern
Political Struggle," Negro Digest, XIX (May, 1970),
5-9.

_____. "Race, Morality and Political Solutions," Phylon,
XX (September, 1959), 242-247.

Hamm, W. C. "Three Phases of Colored Suffrage," North
American Review, 168 (March, 1899), 285-296.

Haworth, P. L. "Disenfranchisement in Louisiana,"
Outlook, 71 (May 17, 1902), 163-166.

Hazel, David W. "An Analysis of Suffrage in the South,"
Negro History Bulletin, X (May, 1947), 182-185.

Hemphill, J. C. "South and the Negro Vote," North American Review, 202 (August, 1915), 213-219.

Henderson, Elmer. "Political Changes Among Negroes in
Chicago During the Depression," Social Forces (May,
1941).

Hilburn, Lincoln C. "California's New Political Force,"
Bronze American (April, 1965).

Hill, D. C. "The Negro as a Political and Social Issue in
the Oregon Country," Journal of Negro History,
XXXIII (April, 1948), 130-141.

Holland, Lynwood M. and Joseph L. Bernd. "Recent
Restrictions Upon Negro Suffrage: The Case of

Georgia," Journal of Politics, XXI (August, 1959), 487-613.

Holloway, Harry. "The Negro and the Vote: The Case of Texas," Journal of Politics, 23 (August, 1961), 526-566.

_____. "The Texas Negro as a Voter," Phylon, XXIV (Summer, 1963), 135-145.

Hurt, H. "Negro Politics," Reporter, XXXV (August 13, 1966), 23-27.

Irving, Florence B. "The Future of the Negro Voter in the South," Journal of Negro Education, XXVII (Summer, 1957), 390-399.

Jackson, Luther P. "The Present Voting Status of the Negroes in the South," Negro History Bulletin, XI (June, 1948), 208-210.

_____. "Race and Suffrage in the South Since 1960," New South, V (June-July, 1948), entire issue.

Jenks, A. E. "Aspects of the Negro Problem," Science, 35 (April 26, 1912), 667-668.

Johnson, James W. "The Gentlemen's Agreement and the Negro Vote," Crisis, XXVIII (October, 1924), 160-164.

_____. "How Should We Vote?" Crisis, XXXV (November, 1928), 368, 386.

_____. "Negro Looks at Politics," American Mercury, 18 (September, 1929), 89-94.

Jordan, Vernon. "The Negro in the Southern Political Process," New South, XXII (Summer, 1967), 82.

Keech, W. R. "The Negro Vote as a Political Resource: The Case of Durham." Unpublished Ph.D. dissertation, University of Wisconsin, 1966.

Kesselman, Louis C. "Negro Voting in a Border Community: Louisville, Kentucky," Journal of Negro Education, XXII (Summer, 1957), 273-280.

King, Mae C. "Politics Southern Style," The Black Politician (July, 1971).

Kopkind, A. "Seat Belts for Mississippi Five," New Republic, 153 (July 24, 1965), 17-18.

Kyle, Keith. "Desegregation and the Negro Right to Vote," Commentary, XXIII (July, 1957), 15-19.

Leggett, John C. "Working Class Consciousness, Race and Political Choice," American Journal of Sociology, LXIX (September, 1963), 171-176.

Lewis, Anthony. "Negro Vote Curbs Exposed by the F.B.I.," New York Times (August 4, 1957).

Lewis, Earl M. "The Negro Voter in Mississippi," Journal of Negro Education, XXVII (Summer, 1957), 329-350.

Lewis, P. F. "Impact of Negro Migration on the Electoral Geography of Flint, Michigan 1932-1962: A Cartographic Analysis," Annals of the Association of American Geographers (March, 1965).

"Limiting Negro Votes: Georgia," Commonweal, 1 (March 14, 1958), 605.

Litchfield, Edward. "A Case Study of Negro Political Behavior in Detroit," Public Opinion Quarterly (June, 1941).

Litwack, Leon. "The Federal Government and the Free Negro," Journal of Negro History (October, 1958), 261-278.

Logan, Rayford W. "The New South, 1959," Quarterly Review of Higher Education Among Negroes, 27 (July, 1959), 149-155.

Lowell, Stanley H. "Votes for Negroes?" The Nation, 158 (April 22, 1944), 470-472.

Lubell, Samuel. "The Future of the Negro Voter in the United States," Journal of Negro Education, XXVII (Summer, 1957), 408-417.

Luce, C. B. "Political Power of the Negro in America,"

McCall's, 92 (November, 1964), 26.

Mabee, C. "Voting in the Black Belt, " Negro History
    Bulletin, 27 (December, 1963), 50-56.

Mabry, William A. "White Supremacy and the North Caro-
    lina Suffrage Amendment, " North Carolina Historical
    Review, XIII (January, 1936), 1-6.

McCain, James T. "The Negro Voter in South Carolina, "
    Journal of Negro Education, XXVII (Summer, 1957),
    359-361.

McGuinn, Henry J. "The Negro Voter in Virginia, "
    Journal of Negro Education, XXVII (Summer, 1957),
    378-389.

McKelway, A. J. "Suffrage in Georgia, " Outlook, 87
    (September 14, 1907), 63-66.

McKinney, William. "The Negro in Pennsylvania Politics, "
    Opportunity, XVII (February, 1939).

McLaughlin, A. C. "Mississippi and the Negro Question, "
    Atlantic Monthly, 70 (December, 1892), 828-837.

Martin, G. A. "Southern Fear and Negro Voting, " Com-
    monweal, 80 (April 24, 1964), 135-137.

Martin, Robert E. "The Relative Political Status of the
    Negro in the United States, " Journal of Negro Edu-
    cation, XXII (Summer, 1953), 363-379.

Matthews, Donald and James W. Prothro. "Negro Voter
    Registration in the South, " in Allan P. Sindler (ed.),
    Change in the Contemporary South (Durham: Duke
    University Press, 1963), 139-149.

_____. _____. "Political Factors and Negro Voter
    Registration in the South, " American Political Science
    Review, LVII (June, 1961), 335-367.

_____. _____. "Social and Economic Factors and
    Negro Voter Registration in the South, " American
    Political Science Review, LVII (March, 1963), 24-44.

Mayo, A. D. "Progress of the Negro, " Forum, 217

(November, 1890), 335-345.

Merritt, Dixon. "Politics and the Southern Negro," Out-
    look, 149 (August 8, 1928), 230-231.

Middlebrooks, A. E. "Alabama Negroes Prepare to Vote,"
    Christian Century, 63 (February 20, 1946), 244.

Miller, J. Erroll. "Major Political Issues Which Directly
    Concern Negroes," Quarterly Review of Higher Edu-
    cation Among Negroes, XVI (October, 1948), 140-
    150.

_____. "The Negro in Present Day Politics with Special
    Reference to Philadelphia, 1882," The Midwest Jour-
    nal (Winter, 1948).

_____. "A Typical Voting Behavior in Philadelphia,"
    The Public Opinion Quarterly (Fall, 1948).

Miller, Kelly. "Government and the Negro," Annals of
    American Academy of Political and Social Science,
    CXL (November, 1928), 98-104.

Milton, D. F. "Black Ballots in the White South," Forum,
    78 (December, 1927), 906-913.

Moon, Henry Lee. "The Negro in Politics," New Republic,
    CXIX (October 18, 1948), 9-10.

_____. "The Negro Vote in the South: 1952," The Na-
    tion, 175 (September 27, 1952), 248-249.

_____. "The Negro Voter," The Nation, 191 (September
    17, 1960), 155-157.

_____. "Politics and the Negro," The Nation, 183 (July
    7, 1956), 11-14.

_____. "The Southern Scene," Phylon, XVI (Winter,
    1955), 351-358.

Morrison, Allan. "Negro Political Progress in New
    England," Ebony, 18 (October, 1963), 25-28.

Morton, Ferdinand. "The Colored Vote," Opportunity, XV
    (March, 1937).

Nabrit, James M. "The Future of the Negro Voter in the
    South," Journal of Negro Education (Summer, 1957),
    418-423.

"Negro Delegates," Nation, 94 (June 20, 1912), 606.

"The Negro in Louisiana Politics," The Sepia Socialite
    (April, 1942).

"Negro in Politics," New Republic, 119 (October 18, 1948),
    9-15.

"Negro Political Action," New Republic, 120 (March 7, 1949),
    29.

"Negro Progress in 1950," Ebony, XIV, No. 3 (January,
    1959), 86-90.

"Negro Progress in 1960," Ebony, XVI, No. 3 (January,
    1961), 82-88.

"Negro Progress in 1961," Ebony, XVII, No. 3 (January,
    1962), 21-28.

"Negro Progress in 1962," Ebony, XVIII, No. 3 (January,
    1963), 84-88.

"Negro Progress in 1964," Ebony, XX, No. 3 (January,
    1965), 107-114.

"Negro Question and its Solution," Independent, 77 (March
    23, 1914), 395-396.

"Negro Suffrage in the South," Outlook, 74 (July 13, 1903),
    399-403.

"Negro to Negroes on Voting," Literary Digest, 109 (April
    25, 1931), 24.

"Negro Vote," Commonweal, 65 (November 16, 1956), 164.

"The Negro Vote in the South," Journal of Negro Education,
    XXVI (September, 1957), entire issue.

"The Negro Vote Trends in the North," Congressional
    Quarterly Weekly Report, 506.

"Negro Voter," New Republic, 130 (June 7, 1954), 51.

"Negro Voter Registration Remains Constant in South," New South (January, 1959), 8-9.

"Negro Voters in the South," Commonweal, 65 (November 9, 1956), 6.

"Negroes and Politics," America, 110 (June 6, 1964), 782.

"Negroes Free Before the Civil War," Negro History Bulletin, I (November, 1937), 2, 6.

"Negroes Vote in Mississippi," Ebony, VII (November, 1951), 15-22.

Newton, I. G. "Expansion of Negro Suffrage in North Carolina," Journal of Negro Education, XXVII (Summer, 1957).

O'Connor, J. J. "Negro Voter in the South," Commonweal, 63 (January 20, 1956), 400-402.

Olbrich, Emil. "The Development of Sentiment on Negro Suffrage to 1860," (Madison: University of Wisconsin Press, 1912).

"Parties and Politics in Harlem," Freedomways, 3, No. 3 (Summer, 1963).

Peters, William. "Race War in Chicago," New Republic, 122 (April 17, 1950), 28.

Poe, C. H. "Suffrage Restrictions in the South," North American Review, 65 (1902), 534.

"Political Gains By Negroes," U.S. News & World Report, 69 (July 13, 1970), 40-41.

"Politics and the Negro," Harper's Weekly, 47 (May 9, 1903), 777.

Price, Hugh D. "The Negro and Florida Politics 1944-1954," Journal of Politics, XVII (May, 1955), 198-220.

_____. "The Negro and Southern Politics," American Journal of Sociology. LXIV (July 1958-May 1959), 325-326.

Price, Margaret. "The Negro Voter in the South, " New South, XII (September, 1957), entire issue.

Rauh, Joseph L., Jr. "Political Participation, " Civil Rights Digest (Summer, 1968), 9-11.

"Reaction with Colonization, " Negro History Bulletin, I (January, 1938), 2-3.

Ready, Elston R. "The Expansion of Negro Suffrage in Florida, " Journal of Education, XXVII (Summer, 1957), 297-306.

"Registration in the South, " Congressional Quarterly Weekly Report, 513.

Reid, Ira De. "Georgia's Negro Vote, " The Nation, 163 (July 6, 1946), 12-14.

Robinson, George F., Jr. "The Negro in Politics in Chicago, " Journal of Negro History, XVII (April, 1932), 180-229.

Rose, John C. "Negro Suffrage: The Constitutional Point of View, " American Political Science Review, I (November, 1906), 17-43.

Rowan, Carl. "Who Gets the Negro Vote?" Look, XX (November 13, 1956), 37-39.

Rustin, Bayard. "Black Power and Coalition Politics, " Commentary, XLVIII (September, 1969), 35-40.

_____. "From Protest to Politics, " Commentary, XXXIX (February, 1965), 25-31.

Salvage, W. S. "Negro in Politics in Kansas and Iowa, " Negro History Bulletin, 25 (February, 1962), 110-111.

Sanders, Charles L. and Poinsett, Alex. "Black Power at the Polls, " Ebony, XXIII, No. 3 (January, 1968), 23-35.

Schurz, C. "Negro in Politics, " Harper's Weekly, 41 (September 4, 1897), 871.

Seasholes, Bradbury and F. Cleaveland. "Negro Political

Participation in Two Piedmont Crescent Cities," in
Frances S. Chapin and Shirley F. Weiss (ed.), Urban
Growth Dynamics (New York: John Wiley & Sons,
1962), 260-308.

Seligman, H. J. "Negroes Influence as a Voter," Current
History, 28 (May, 1928), 230-231.

Sheeler, J. Reuben. "The Struggle of the Negro in Ohio
for Freedom," Journal of Negro History, XXXI, No.
2 (April, 1946).

Shugg, Roger. "Negro Voting in the Ante-bellum South,"
Journal of Negro History, XXI (October, 1936), 357-
364.

Sigel, Roberta. "Race and Religion as Factors in the
Kennedy Victory in Detroit, 1960," Journal of Negro
Education, XXXI (Fall, 1962), 436-447.

Sindler, Allan P. "Protest Against the Political Status of
the Negro," The Annals (January, 1965), 48-54.

Smith, Wilfred H. "The Disfranchisement of the Negro,"
Alexander Magazine, I (May 15, 1905), 17-19.

Smith, William G. "The Status of the Negro," New Republic, 122 (April 17, 1950), 28.

"Southern Justice to the Negro," Outlook, 98 (June 17,
1911), 317-318.

"The Southern Negro: 1952." The Nation, 175 (September
27,1952), 243-245.

Spicer, G. W. "The Federal Judiciary and Political Change
in the South," Journal of Politics, XXVI (February,
1964), 154-176.

Steinberg, C. "The Southern Negro's Right to Vote,"
American Federationists, LXIX (July, 1962), 1-6.

Stony, George C. "Suffrage in the South, Part I--The Poll
Tax," Survey Graphics, XXIX (January, 1940), 5-9.

Strong, Donald S. "The Future of the Negro Voter in the
South," Journal of Negro Education, XXVII (Summer,
1957), 400-407.

_____. "Rise of Negro Voting in Texas," American
Political Science Review, 42 (June, 1948), 310-322.

_____. "The Rise of Negro Voting in Texas," in
Arnold M. Rose, Race, Prejudice and Discrimination (New York, 1951).

Stroud, Virgil. "The Negro Voter in the South," Quarterly
Review of Higher Education Among Negroes, 29
(January, 1961), 9-39.

_____. "Voter Registration in North Carolina," Journal
of Negro Education (Spring, 1961), 153-155.

Sweat, Edward F. "Social Status of the Free Negro in
Antebellum Georgia," Negro History Bulletin, XXI
(March, 1958), 129-131.

_____. "State and Local Politics in 1968," in P. Romero
(ed.), Black American (Washington, D.C.: United
Publishing Corporation, 1969), 133-146.

Taper, Bernard. "A Break with Tradition," New Yorker,
XLI (June 24, 1965), 68.

Tatum, Elbert L. "The Changed Political Thought of the
Negroes in the United States, 1915-1940," Journal
of Negro Education, XVI (Fall, 1947), 50, 522-533.

Taylor, A. A. "The Negro in the Reconstruction of
Virginia," Journal of Negro History, XI (April,
1926), 243-415; (July, 1926), 425-537.

_____. "The Negro in South Carolina During the Re-
construction," Journal of Negro History, IX (July,
1924), 241-346; (October, 1924), 381-569.

"Texas Statute Forbidding Negroes to Vote in Primaries
Declared Unconstitutional," Congressional Digest, 6
(April, 1927), 139.

Toppin, Edgar A. "Negro Emancipation in Historic Retrospect: Ohio: The Negro Suffrage Issue in Postbel-
lum Ohio Politics," Journal of Human Relations, XI
(Winter, 1963), 252-286.

Valien, Preston. "Expansion of Negro Suffrage in

Tennessee," Journal of Negro Education, XXVII
(Summer, 1957), 362-368.

Van Deusen, John G. "The Negro in Politics," Journal of
Negro History, XXI (July, 1936), 256-274.

Walker, Jack. "Negro Voting in Atlanta, 1953-1961,"
Phylon, XIV (Winter, 1963), 378-387.

Wall, Marvin. "Black Votes," South Today (August, 1961),
6-7.

Walton, Hanes, Jr. "Black Politics in the South," Ebony,
XXVI No. 10 (August, 1971), 140-143.

Walton, L. S. "Negro in Politics," Outlook, 137 (July 23,
1924), 472-473.

Ward, Paul W. "Wooing the Negro Vote," The Nation, 143
(August 1, 1936), 119-120.

Wardlow, Ralph W. "Negro Suffrage in Georgia 1867-1930,"
(Athens: Phelps-Stoke, 1932).

Washington, B. T. "Progress of the Negro in One County
in the South," Outlook, 81 (December 8, 1905), 874-
875.

Watson, T. E. "Negro Question in the South," Arena, 61
(October, 1892), 540-550.

Watters, Pat. "The Negro Enters Southern Politics,"
Dissent, XIII (July-August, 1966), 365-367.

_____. "Negro Registration in the South," New Republic,
150 (April 4, 1964), 15-17.

_____. "Negro's Strategies in the South," Dissent (July-
August, 1966), 361-368.

Weeks, S. B. "History of Negro Suffrage in the South,"
Political Science Quarterly (December, 1894), 671-
703.

Wesley, Charles H. "The Emancipation of the Free Colored
Population," Journal of Negro History, XIX, No. 2
(April, 1934.)

_____. "The Negro's Struggle for Freedom in its Birth-place," Journal of Negro History, XXX, No. 1 (January, 1945).

White, H. "Disfranchising the Negro in Mississippi and Georgia," Nation, 69 (November 23, 1899), 384-385.

"White Primary in Atlanta," Time, 44 (July 17, 1944), 22.

Wilkins, Roy. "The Future of the Negro Voter in the United States," Journal of Negro Education, XXVII (Summer, 1967), 424.

_____. "An Interview with Louisiana's Kingfish," Crisis, XLII (February, 1935), 41-55.

Wilson, James Q. "The Changing Political Posture of the Negro," in Arnold Rose (ed.), Assuring Freedom to the Free (Detroit: Wayne State University Press, 1964), 163-184.

_____. "How the Northern Negro Uses His Vote," Reporter, XXII (March 31, 1960), 11-12.

_____. "The Negro in American Politics: The Present," in John Davis (ed.), American Negro Reference Book (New York: Prentice-Hall, 1965), 431-457.

_____. "Two Negro Politicians: An Interpretation," Midwest Journal of Political Science, IV (November, 1960), 360-369.

Wolfe, Deborah Partridge. "Negroes in American Politics," Negro Educational Review, XIV (April, 1963), 64-71.

Woodson, Carter G. "The Negro in Maryland," Negro History Bulletin, XII (June, 1949), 207-214.

_____. "The Negro in Pennsylvania," Negro History Bulletin, XIII (April, 1949), 150-152.

Wright, Marion T. "Negro Suffrage in New Jersey, 1776-1875," Journal of Negro History, XXXIII (April, 1948), 108-122.

Wright, T. Morris. "The First Colored Voter of Kentucky," The Colored American Magazine (February, 1901), 292-293.

Zinn, Howard. "Registration in Alabama, " New Republic, CXLIX (October 26, 1963), 11-12.

Dissertations

Bacote, Clarence A. The Negro in Georgia Politics, 1880-1908. University of Chicago, 1956.

Bancroft, Frederic. A Sketch of the Negro in Politics, Especially in South Carolina and Mississippi. Columbia University, 1885.

Barnes, James F. Negro Voting in Mississippi. University of Mississippi, 1955.

Bond, J. Max. The Negro in Los Angeles. University of Southern California, 1936.

Boucher, Morris R. The Free Negro in Alabama Prior to 1860. University of Iowa, 1950.

Bowman, Robert L. Negro Politics in Four Southern Counties. University of North Carolina, 1964.

Brittain, Joseph M. Negro Suffrage and Politics in Alabama Since 1870. Indiana University, 1958.

Buni, Andrew. The Negro in Virginia Politics, 1902-1950. University of Virginia, 1965.

Cavanagh, Helen M. Anti-Slavery Sentiment and Politics in the Northwest, 1844-1860. University of Chicago, 1938.

Cobb, Henry E. Negroes in Alabama During the Reconstruction Period, 1865-1875. Temple University, 1953.

Cohen, Leon S. The Southern Negro: A Model of Ethnic Political Assimilation. University of North Carolina, 1965.

Collins, Ernest M. The Political Behavior of the Negroes in Cincinnati, Ohio and Louisville, Kentucky. University of Kentucky, 1950.

Corlew, Robert E. The Negro in Tennessee, 1870-1900.
    University of Alabama, 1954.

Edmonds, Helen G. The Negro and Fusion Politics in North
    Carolina, 1895-1901. Ohio State University, 1946.

England, James M. The Free Negro in Antebellum Ten-
    nessee. Vanderbilt University, 1941.

Farris, Charles D. Effects of Negro Voting Upon the
    Politics Of a Southern City: An Intensive Study,
    1946-48. University of Chicago, 1953.

Fishel, Leslie H., Jr. The North and the Negro, 1865-
    1900: A Study in Race Discrimination. Harvard
    University, 1954.

Fuller, Luther M. The Negro in Boston, 1864-1954.
    Columbia University, 1956.

Gelb, Joyce. The Role of Negro Politicians in the Demo-
    cratic, Republican and Liberal Parties of New York
    City. New York University, 1969.

Gooden, John E. Negro Participation in Civil Government
    with Emphasis on Public Education in Texas. Uni-
    versity of Southern California, 1950.

Kifer, Allen F. The Negro Under the New Deal, 1933-1941.
    University of Wisconsin, 1961.

Logan, Frenise A. The Negro in North Carolina, 1876-
    1894. Western Reserve University, 1954.

Mabry, William A. The Disfranchisement of the Negro in
    the South. Duke University, 1933.

McConnell, Roland C. The Negro in North Carolina Since
    Reconstruction. New York University, 1945.

Meier, August. Negro Racial Thought in the Age of Booker
    T. Washington, circa 1880-1915. Columbia Univer-
    sity, 1957.

Miller, James E. The Negro in Pennsylvania Politics with
    Special Reference to Philadelphia Since 1932. Uni-
    versity of Pennsylvania, 1946.

Morsell, John A. The Political Behavior of Negroes in
    New York City. Columbia University, 1956.

Neyland, Leedell W. The Negro in Louisiana Since 1900:
    An Economic and Social Study. New York University,
    1959.

Richardson, Joe M. The Negro in the Reconstruction of
    Florida. Florida State University, 1963.

Robert, Cleo. Some Correlates of Registration and Voting
    Among Negroes in the 1953 Municipal Election of
    Atlanta. Atlanta University, 1954.

Scheiner, Seth M. The Negro in New York City, 1865-1910.
    New York University, 1963.

Seasholes, Bradbury. Negro Political Participation in Two
    North Carolina Cities. University of North Caro-
    lina, 1962.

Sheeler, John R. The Negro in West Virginia Before 1900.
    University of West Virginia, 1954.

Solomon, Thomas R. Participation of Negroes in Detroit
    Elections. University of Michigan, 1939.

Starland, Victor D. Factors Associated with Negro Voting
    in a Delta County of Arkansas. University of Ar-
    kansas, 1961.

Webb, Allie B. W. A History of Negro Voting in Louisiana,
    1877-1906. Louisiana State University, 1962.

Wharton, Vernon L. The Negro in Mississippi 1865-1890.
    University of North Carolina, 1940.

Whitaker, Hugh S. A New Day: The Effects of Negro En-
    franchisement in Selected Mississippi Counties.
    Florida State University, 1965.

Wilhoit, Francis M. The Politics of Desegregation in
    Georgia. Harvard University, 1958.

Williamson, Joel R. The Negro in South Carolina During
    Reconstruction, 1861-1877. Berkeley, University of
    California, 1964.

Books

Aiken, Charles. The Negro Votes. San Francisco:
    Chandler Publishing Company, 1962.

Allen, James Egert. The Negro in New York. New York:
    Exposition, 1964.

Bailey, Harry Jr. Negro Politics in America. Cleveland:
    Charles Merrill, 1968.

Buni, Andrew. The Negro in Virginia Politics 1902-1965.
    Charlottesville: University of Virginia Press, 1967.

Calcott, Margaret Law. The Negro in Maryland Politics
    1870-1912. Baltimore: The Johns Hopkins Press,
    1969.

Edmonds, Helen. The Negro and Fusion Politics in North
    Carolina--1894-1900. Chapel Hill: University of
    North Carolina Press, 1951.

Farmer, James. Freedom When? New York: Random
    House, 1966.

Gillette, William. The Right to Vote: Politics and the
    Passage of the Fifteenth Amendment. Baltimore:
    Johns Hopkins Press, 1968.

Gosnell, Harold. Negro Politicians: The Rise of Negro
    Politics in Chicago. Chicago: University of Chicago
    Press, 1935.

Grier, William H. and Price M. Cobbs. Black Rage. New
    York: Basic Books, Inc., 1968.

Hamilton, Charles V. Minority Politics in Black Belt
    Alabama. New York: McGraw-Hill, 1962.

_____. and Stokely Carmichael. Black Power: The
    Politics of Liberation in America. New York:
    Random House, 1967.

Hentoff, Nat. The New Equality. New York: Viking Press,
    1964.

Hovan, James D. The Seat of Power. New York: Crown
    Publishers, 1965.

Key, V. O., Jr. Southern Politics in State and Nation.
    Gloucester, Mass.: Peter Smith, 1949.

Lewinson, Paul. Race, Class and Party: A History of
    Negro Suffrage and White Politics in the South.
    New York: Russell and Russell, 1963.

Lloyd, R. G. White Supremacy in the United States.
    Washington, D.C.: Public Affairs Press, 1952.

Logan, Rayford W. The Negro in American Life and
    Thought: The Nadir 1877-1901. New York: Dial
    Press, Inc., 1954.

Mabry, William. Studies in the Disfranchisement of the
    Negro in the South. Durham: Duke University
    Press, 1938.

Moon, Henry Lee. Balance of Power: The Negro Vote.
    New York: Doubleday, 1948.

Morton, R. L. The Negro in Virginia Politics. Charlottes-
    ville: University of Virginia Press, 1919.

Nowlin, William F. The Negro in American National
    Politics. Boston: Stratford, 1931.

Ogden, Frederick D. The Poll Tax in the South. Univer-
    sity: University of Alabama Press, 1958.

Porter, Kirk. A History of Suffrage in the United States.
    Chicago: University of Chicago Press, 1919.

Price, Hugh D. The Negro and Southern Politics. New
    York: New York University Press, 1957.

Price, Margaret. The Negro and the Ballot in the South.
    Atlanta: Southern Regional Council, 1959.

_____. The Negro Voter in the South. Atlanta: Southern
    Regional Council, 1957.

Shadgett, Olive H. Voter Registration in Georgia: A Study
    of its Administration. Athens: Bureau of Public Ad-
    ministration, University of Georgia, 1955.

Silberman, Charles E. Crisis in Black and White. New

York: Random House, 1964.

Silverman, Sondra (ed.). The Black Revolt and Democratic
    Politics. Massachusetts: D. C. Heath and Com-
    pany, 1970.

Smith, Stanley and Lewis Jones. Tuskegee, Alabama Voting
    Rights and Economic Pressure. New York: Anti-
    Defamation League, 1958.

Spangler, Earl. The Negro in Minnesota. Minneapolis:
    T. S. Denison & Company, Inc., 1961.

Stampp, Kenneth M. The Era of Reconstruction. New
    York: Alfred A. Knopf, 1965.

Stone, Chuck. Black Political Power in America.
    Indianapolis: Bobbs-Merrill, 1968.

_____. Tell It Like It Is. New York: Trident Press,
    1967.

Strong, Donald S. Negroes, Ballots and Judges. Univer-
    sity: University of Alabama Press, 1968.

_____. Registration of Voters in Alabama. University:
    Bureau of Public Administration, University of
    Alabama, 1956.

Taper, Bernard. Gomillion versus Lightfoot: The Tuskegee
    Gerrymander Case. New York: McGraw-Hill, 1962.

Tatum, Elbert L. The Changed Political Thought of the
    Negro, 1915-1940. New York: Exposition Press,
    1941.

United States Commission on Civil Rights. Political Par-
    ticipation. Washington, D.C.: U.S. Government
    Printing Office, 1968.

Walton, Hanes, Jr. The Political Philosophy of Martin
    Luther King, Jr. Connecticut: Greenwood Publish-
    ing Company, 1971.

Watters, Pat and Reese Cleghorn. Climbing Jacob's
    Ladder: The Arrival of Negroes in Southern Politics.
    New York: Harcourt, Brace and World, Inc., 1970.

Wish, Harvey (ed.). The Negro Since Emancipation. New
    York: Prentice-Hall, 1964.

Young, Whitney M., Jr. To Be Equal. New York:
    McGraw-Hill Book Company, 1964.

BLACK NEWSPAPERS

Articles

Bayton, J. A. and E. Bell. "An Exploratory Study of the
    Role of the Negro Press," Journal of Negro Educa-
    tion, 20 (Winter, 1951), 8-15.

Beard, Richard L. and Cyril E. Zoerner. "Associated
    Negro Press: Its Founding, Ascendency and Demise,"
    Journalism Quarterly, 46 (Spring, 1969), 47-52.

Bennett, Lerone, Jr. "Founder of the Negro Press,"
    Ebony, 19 (July, 1964), 96-98+ .

Hirsch, Paul M. "An Analysis of Ebony; The Magazine
    and its Readers," Journalism Quarterly, 45 (Summer,
    1968), 261-270.

Logan, Rayford W. "Attitude of the Southern Press Toward
    Negro Suffrage," Quarterly Review of Higher Educa-
    tion Among Negroes, 8 (July, 1940), 180.

McAlpin, H. "Negro Press and Politics," New Republic, 111
    (October 16, 1944), 493.

McCombs, Maxwell E. "Negro Use of Television and News-
    papers for Political Information, 1952-1964," Journal
    of Broadcasting, 12 (Summer, 1968), 261-266.

"Negro Press Marks 135th Anniversary," Editor and Pub-
    lisher, 95 (March 17, 1962), 13.

Pride, Armistead Scott. "An Untold Story in American
    Journalism: The Negro Newspaper," Negro Educa-
    tional Review, II (April, 1951), 60-64.

Rosche, Bernard. "The Negro Press Views the Riots,"
    Interplay, I (February, 1968), 9-11.

Thornbrough, Emma Lou. "American Negro Newspapers, 1880-1914," Business Historical Review, 40 (First Quarter, 1966), 467-490.

Waters, Enoch P. "The Negro Press: A Call for Change," Editor and Publisher, 95 (May 12, 1962), 67-68.

Dissertations

Brooks, Maxwell R. Content Analysis of Leading Negro Newspapers. Ohio State University, 1953.

Brown, Warren. Social Change and the Negro Press, 1860-1880. New School for Social Research, 1950.

Fenderson, Lewis H. Development of the Negro Press, 1827-1948. University of Pittsburgh, 1949.

Jones, Wendell P. The Negro Press and the Higher Education of Negroes, 1933-1952: A Study of News and Opinion on Higher Education in the Three Leading Negro Newspapers. University of Chicago, 1954.

Pride, Armistead S. A Register and History of Negro Newspapers in the United States, 1827-1950. Northwestern University, 1950.

Reddick, Lawrence D. The Negro in the New Orleans Press, 1850-1860: A Study in Attitudes and Propaganda. University of Chicago, 1939.

Simpson, George E. The Negro in the White Newspapers of Philadelphia. University of Pennsylvania, 1934.

Books

Brooks, Maxwell. The Negro Press Re-Examined: Political Content of Leading Negro Newspapers. Boston: Christopher Publishing House, 1959.

Detweiler, Frederick G. The Negro Press in the United States. Chicago: University of Chicago Press, 1922.

Fisher, Paul and Ralph Lowenstein, eds. Race and News Media. New York: Praeger, 1967.

Gore, George William, Jr. Negro Journalism: An Essay on the History and Present Condition of the Negro Press. Greencastle, 1922.

Hill, Roy L. Who's Who in the American Negro Press. Dallas: Royal Publishing Company, 1960.

Kerlin, Robert T. The Voice of the Negro. New York: E. P. Dutton Company, 1920.

Logan, Rayford (ed.). The Attitudes of the Southern White Press Toward Negro Suffrage, 1932-1940. Washington: Foundation Publishers, 1940.

Lyle, Jack, ed. The Black American and the Press. Los Angeles: Ward Ritchie, 1968.

Oak, Vishnu V. The Negro Newspaper. Yellow Springs, Ohio: Antioch Press, 1948.

Penn, I. Garland. The Afro-American Press and Its Editors. Springfield, Massachusetts: Willey, 1891.

Schuyler, George S. Fifty Years of Progress in Negro Journalism. Pittsburgh, Pennsylvania: Pittsburgh Courier Publishing Company, 1950.

Simpson, George Eaton. The Negro in the Philadelphia Press. Philadelphia: University of Pennsylvania, 1936.

Chapter VIII

BLACKS AND POLITICAL SCIENCE METHODOLOGY

The models and techniques which white political science developed to study the American political process and other aspects of politics have for the most part been applied to the study of black politics.

Mack Jones' A Frame of Reference for Black Politics and his paper on "The White Custodians of the Black Experience," done in conjunction with Professor Alex Willingham, were pioneering and seminal efforts to develop a frame of reference appropriate for the black experience.

Coupled with Jones and Willingham's efforts to forge a new path has been that of Greenberg, who in an essay entitled "Models of the Political Process of Studying American Politics: Implications for the Black Community" [See, Edward S. Greenberg, Neal Milner and D. Olson (eds), Black Politics (New York: Holt, Rinehart and Winston, 1971), pp. 3-15], criticized the pluralist and elite models as poor methodological tools for looking at the black experience. Greenberg's work was the first, along with Samuel Cook's article, "The American Liberal Democratic Tradition of the Black Revolution and Martin Luther King, Jr.," and Hanes Walton, Jr.'s The Political Philosophy of Martin Luther King, Jr., to point out the inappropriateness of white-oriented schemes and methodology.

Much more needs to be done in this area, and con-

flict over the correct type of methodology can be expected
to emerge in the future.

Articles and Dissertations

Bennett, Lerone, Jr.   "The Politics of the Outsider," Negro
    Digest (July, 1968), 5-8.

Calhoun, Herbert L.   "Methodology for Environmental Pro-
    jections," Douglas A /C.

_____.   "The 'Source' Model," Northrop A /C.

Cnuddle, Charles.   "Consensus, Rules of the Game and
    Democratic Politics: The Case of Race Politics in
    the South."   Unpublished Ph.D. dissertation, Uni-
    versity of North Carolina, 1967, Chapter 1-2.

Cook, Samuel DuBois.   "The American Liberal Tradition,
    the Black Revolution and Martin Luther King, Jr."
    Introduction to: Hanes Walton, Jr., The Political
    Philosophy of Martin Luther King, Jr.   (Connecticut:
    Greenwood Publishing Co., 1971).

_____.   "The Classical Conception of Political Education
    with Special Reference to Plato," Review of Higher
    Education Among Negroes, XXIX (1961).

Ince, Basil A.   "Politics, Political Scientists and Trends in
    the Field," Reader in Political Science (January,
    1970).

Jones, Mack.   "A Framework for the Study of Black Poli-
    tics."   A Paper read at the 1969 Southern Political
    Science Convention (November 6-8, 1969), Miami,
    Florida.

Murapa, Rukudze.   "Race, Pride and Black Political Thought,"
    Negro Digest, XVII (May, 1969), 6-9.

Patterson, Beeman.   "The Politics of Recognition: Negro
    Politics in Los Angeles," Unpublished Ph.D. disser-
    tation. University of California, 1969, Chapter 6.

Prestage, Jewel. "Black Politics and the Kerner Report:
    Consensus and Directions," Social Science Quarterly
    (December, 1968), 462-464.

Strange, John. "The Negro in Philadelphia Politics, 1963-
    1965." Unpublished Ph.D. dissertation.
    Princeton University, 1966, Chapter 9.

Books

Bailey, Harry A., Jr. Ethnic Group Politics. Columbus,
    Ohio: Charles E. Merrill Books, 1969.

Holloway, Harry. The Politics of the Southern Negro: From
    Exclusion to Big City Organization. New York:
    Random House, 1969. Chapter 1.

Prothro, James and Donald Matthews. Negroes and the New
    Southern Politics. New York: Harcourt, Brace and
    World, 1966. Chapter 2.

Chapter IX

BLACK POLITICAL THOUGHT

At this writing there is no book or essay which covers all the black political thinkers. There are two readers on the political writing of black leaders but no full scholarly analysis of black political thinkers exists. The need for this was outlined in a book review essay by Professor Hanes Walton, Jr. entitled "Black Political Thought: The Problem of Characterization," in Journal of Black Studies (December, 1970), which set the parameters of what has to be done.

In his pioneering and seminal work, The Political Philosophy of Martin Luther King, Jr., Professor Walton tried to develop a methodology for the study of black thinkers. The only other work to arrive since that book has been The Political Philosophy of James Forman, which is an edited volume of his speeches.

Needed still are a typology and a comprehensive study of all the black thinkers in the field. Professor Alex Willingham is attempting the latter in his doctoral dissertation to be presented shortly to the University of North Carolina. As for the former, several graduate students at Atlanta University, in the spring of 1972, tried to develop a typology and produced some useful papers.

BLACK POLITICAL LEADERSHIP

Articles and Dissertations

Athey, Louis L. "Florence Kelly and the Quest for Negro Equality," Negro History Bulletin, LVI, No. 4 (October, 1971).

"Black Voices of the South," Ebony, XXVI, No. 10 (August, 1971), 50-54.

Booker, Simeon. "Robert C. Weaver," Ebony, XXI, No. 6 (April, 1966).

Broderick, Francis L. "W. E. B. DuBois: The Trail of His Ideas." Doctoral dissertation, Harvard University, 1955.

Brooks, Albert. "Organizing Negro Leadership," Negro History Bulletin, VIII (May, 1945), 180.

Cheek, William F., III. "Forgotten Prophet: The Life of John Mercer Langston." Doctoral dissertation, University of Virginia, 1961.

Clarke, John. "Malcolm X: The Man and His Time," Negro Digest, XVIII (May, 1969).

Coleman, Charles. Negro Political Leadership During the Reconstruction Period. M.A. thesis, Howard University, 1932.

Cook, Samuel DuBois. "Is Martin Luther King, Jr. Irrelevant?" The New South (Summer, 1971).

"Dangers of Political Leadership," Negro History Bulletin, X (November, 1946), 48.

Davis, Ossie. "Nat Turner: Hero Reclaimed," Freedomways, 8, No. 3 (Summer, 1968).

"Dean of Negro Leaders," Ebony, XXV, No. 1 (November, 1958), 103.

Dreer, Herman. "Negro Leadership in St. Louis: A Study in Race Relations." Doctoral dissertation, University of Chicago, 1956.

Editorial. "Nobel Peace Prize Goes to Martin Luther King,"
    Negro History Bulletin, XXVIII (November, 1969), 35.

Eisenberg, Bernard. "Kelly Miller: The Negro Leader as
    a Marginal Man," Journal of Negro History, XLV,
    No. 3 (July, 1960).

Fladeland, Betty L. "James Gillespie Birney: Exponent of
    Political Action Against Slavery." Doctoral disserta-
    tion, University of Michigan, 1952.

Gill, Robert L. "The Crusading Spirit of Robert C. Weaver,"
    Negro Educational Review, II (July-October, 1951), 120-
    128.

_____. "Jesse O. Thomas--A Pioneer in Public Service,"
    The Phylon (Spring, 1948).

_____. "Robert C. Weaver--A Pioneer in Public Service,"
    The Lincoln University Journal (Spring, 1948).

Giovanni, Nikki. "Malcolm X: The Man and His Times,"
    Freedomways, 10, No. 1 (1970).

Golden, L. Hanga and O. Melikian. "William E. B. DuBois:
    Scientist and Public Figure," Journal of Human Rela-
    tions, XIV (Fall, 1966), 156-168.

Green, K. W. "Miller Fulton Whitaker," Negro Educational
    Review, I (April, 1950), 70-72.

Hale, Frank W. "Frederick Douglass; Anti-Slavery Cru-
    sader and Lecturer," Journal of Human Relations,
    XIV (Fall, 1966), 100-117.

Hare, Nathan. "Why Negro 'Leaders' Lack Power?" Negro
    Digest, XIV (January, 1965).

Henderson, Lenneal J., Jr. "Engineers of Liberation,"
    The Black Politician (Spring, 1970).

_____. "W. E. B. DuBois, Black Scholar and Prophet,"
    The Black Scholar (January, 1970).

Holt, Len W. "A Southern Lawyer Speaks of Freedom,"
    Freedomways, 2, No. 2 (Spring, 1962).

Johnson, Robert B. "The Nature of the Minority Community: Internal Structure, Reactions, Leadership and Action." Doctoral dissertation, Cornell University, 1955.

Ladd, Everett C., Jr. "Agony of the Negro Leader," The Nation, 199 (September 7, 1964), 88-91.

_____. "Negro Political Leadership in the Urban South." Doctoral dissertation, Cornell University, 1964.

Lee, Carleton L. "Patterns of Leadership in Race Relations: A Study of Leadership Among Negro Americans." Doctoral dissertation, University of Chicago, 1951.

McIlinson, Irvin C. "Negro Lawyers in Mississippi," Journal of Negro History, XV, No. 1 (January, 1930).

Mays, Benjamin E. "What's Wrong with Negro Leaders?" Negro Digest, IX (January, 1951).

Miller, Henry. "W. E. B. DuBois; From Plexus," Journal of Human Relations, XIV (Fall, 1966), 131-136.

Murapa, Rukudze. "Race Pride in Black Political Thought," The Negro Digest (May, 1969.

Ottley, Roi. "The Big Ten Who Run Negro America," Negro Digest, VI (May, 1948).

Penty, George and James Crown. "Southern Negro Leader," The Nation, 175 (September 27, 1962), 265-267.

Quarles, Benjamin. "Black Builders of the American Republic," Negro Digest, XIV (February, 1965).

Rowan, Carl T. "Crisis in Civil Rights Leadership," Ebony, XXII, No. 1 (November, 1966).

Talley, T. H. "Marcus Garvey, the Negro Moses?" World's Work, 41 (December, 1920), 153-166.

Tillman, Nathaniel P. "Walter Francis White: A Study in Interest Group Leadership." Doctoral dissertation,

University of Wisconsin, 1961.

Thompson, Daniel C. "The Negro Leadership Class,"
     American Journal of Sociology, 242-243.

Walker, Jack L., Jr. "Protest and Negotiation: A Study
     of Negro Political Leaders in a Southern City."
     Doctoral dissertation, State University of Iowa, 1903.

Walton, Hanes, Jr. "The Political Leadership of Martin
     Luther King," Quarterly Review of Higher Education
     Among Negroes, 36 (July, 1968), 163-171.

Wilson, Charles T. "Triumph in Leadership Tragedy," in
     John Hendrik Clarke, Malcolm X, The Man and His
     Times (Macmillan, 1969).

Wilson, James Q. "Negro Leaders in Chicago." Doctoral
     dissertation, University of Chicago, 1960.

Young, Richard. "The Impact of Protest Leadership on
     Negro Politicians in San Francisco Co.," Western
     Political Quarterly, 22 (March, 1960), 94-111.

Books

Brotz, Howard. Negro Social and Political Thought, 1850-
     1920. New York: Basic Books, Inc., 1966.

Burgess, M. Elaine. Negro Leadership in a Southern City.
     New Haven, Connecticut: College and University
     Press, 1965.

Foner, Philip (ed.). Frederick Douglass: Selections from
     His Writings. New York: International, 1945.

_____. The Life and Writings of Frederick Douglass.
     4 volumes. New York: International, 1950.

Hedgeman, Annan Arnold. The Trumpet Sounds: A Memoir
     of Negro Leadership. New York: Holt, Rinehart and
     Winston, 1964.

Ladd, Everett C., Jr. Negro Political Leadership in the
     South. Ithaca: Cornell University Press, 1966.

Rollins, Charlemae Hill. They Showed the Way: Forty
    American Negro Leaders. New York: Thomas
    Crowell Company, 1964.

Rudwick, Elliott. W. E. B. DuBois, A Study in Minority
    Group Leadership. Philadelphia: University of
    Pennsylvania Press, 1960.

_____. W. E. B. DuBois: Propagandist of the Negro
    Protest. New York: Atheneum Press, 1968.

Thompson, Daniel C. The Negro Leadership Class. Engle-
    wood Cliffs, New Jersey: Prentice-Hall, 1963.

Warren, Robert Penn. Who Speaks for the Negro. New
    York: Random House, 1965.

Wilson, James Q. Negro Politics: The Search for Leader-
    ship. Glencoe, Illinois: Free Press, 1960.

Young, Margaret B. Black American Leaders. New York:
    Franklin Watts, Inc., 1969.

BLACK POLITICAL REVOLUTIONARY MOVEMENTS

Articles and Dissertations

Abramowitz, Jack. "Accommodation and Militancy in Negro
    Life 1876-1916." Doctoral dissertation, Columbia
    University, 1950.

Aptheker, Herbert. "American Negro Slave Revolts."
    Doctoral dissertation, Columbia University, 1944.

Bennett, Lerone, Jr. "Black Power," Ebony, 21 (February,
    1966), 127-130; (April, 1966), 121-124; (July, 1966),
    58-60; (October, 1966), 152-154; (December, 1966),
    146-148; (January, 1967), 114-116.

_____. "Black Power in Dixie During Reconstruction of
    the South," Ebony, 17 (July, 1962), 84-90.

_____. "Black Power: Reconstruction of the South,

1867-1877, " Ebony, 21 (November, 1965), 28-29;
(December, 1965), 51-52; (January, 1966), 116-122.

"Black Power," New Republic, 154 (June 18, 1966), 5-6.

Bond, Horace Julian.   "The Southern Youth Movement, "
    Freedomways, 2, No. 3 (Summer, 1962).

Brisbane, Robert H., Jr.   "The Rise of Protest Movements
    Among Negroes Since 1900." Doctoral dissertation,
    Harvard University, 1949.

Coney, Alain Burroughs.   "The Revolt of Negro Youth, "
    Freedomways, 1, No. 2 (Summer, 1961).

Contee, Clarence G.   "The Emergence of DuBois as an
    African Nationalist, " Journal of Negro History, LIV,
    No. 1 (January, 1969).

Conyers, John.   "Politics and the Black Revolution, " Ebony,
    XXIV, No. 10 (August, 1969), 162-166.

Cook, Samuel DuBois.   "Political Movements and Organiza-
    tions in the South, " Journal of Politics, XXVI (1964).

DuBois, W. E. B.   "National Committee on the Negro, "
    Survey, 22 (June 12, 1909), 407-409.

Essien-Udom, Essien.   "Black Nationalism: The Search for
    An Identity." Doctoral dissertation, University of
    Chicago, 1962.

Gill, Robert.   "Shaping the Negro Revolution Through Court
    Decisions, 1964-1966, " Journal of Human Relations,
    XV (Summer, 1967), 423-437.

Henderson, George.   "Legal Aspirations and Successes in
    the American Negro Revolution, " Journal of Human
    Relations, XIII (Winter, 1965), 185-194.

Hoffman, E. D.   "The Genesis of the Modern Movement
    for Equal Rights in South Carolina, 1930-1939, "
    Journal of Negro History (October, 1959), 346-369.

Mkalimoto, Ernie.   "The Cultural Arms of Revolutionary
    Black Nationalism, " Negro Digest, XIX (December,
    1969).

O'Dell, Eugene. "The Contours of the 'Black Revolution' in the 1970's," Freedomways, 10, No. 2 (1970).

Ofari, Earl. "The Roots of Black Radicalism," Negro Digest, XVIII (August, 1969).

_____. "W. E. B. DuBois and Black Power," Negro Digest, XIX (December, 1969).

Relyea, Harold C. "Black Power: The Genesis and Future of a Revolution," Journal of Human Relations, XVI (Summer, 1968), 502-512.

Rustin, Bayard. "Black Power and Coalition Politics," Commentary, 42 (September, 1966), 35-40.

Sayler, Edward. "Negro Minority Group Strategy as a Social Movement." Doctoral dissertation, Ohio State University, 1948.

"Youth, Nonviolence and Social Changes," Negro Digest, XIII (March, 1964).

Books

Barbour, Floyd B. (ed.). The Black Power Revolt. Boston: Porter Sargent, 1968.

Brink, William J. The Negro Revolution in America. New York: Simon & Schuster, 1964.

Broderick, Francis L. and Meier, August (eds.). Negro Protest Thought in the Twentieth Century. Indianapolis: Bobbs-Merrill, 1965.

Carmichael, Stokely and Charles V. Hamilton. Black Power: The Politics of Liberation in America. New York: Random House, 1967.

Lofton, John. Insurrection in South Carolina: The Turbulent World of Denmark Vesey. Kent, Ohio: Kent State University Press, 1964.

McPherson, James M. The Negro's Civil War. New York: Pantheon Books, 1965.

Meier, August. Negro Thought in America 1800-1915:
        Racial Ideologies in the Age of Booker T. Washington.
        Ann Arbor: University of Michigan Press, 1963.

Westin, Alan F. (ed.). Freedom Now! The Civil Rights
        Struggle in America. New York: Basic Books, Inc.,
        1964.

Chapter X

BLACKS AND INTERNATIONAL POLITICS

The field of international politics and its relationship to black political activities is one of the most unexplored realms of black politics. A great deal of the current literature is focused upon the third world and its relationship, on the basis of color, to black Americans.

Colonialism and the economic connection are also emerging productive areas in the literature, and can be expected to expand considerably. At present, no comprehensive work is available and none is in the immediate offing, but the need and the demand are so pressing that they should lead to a major work in this area before long.

PAN AFRICAN

Articles

Bunche, Ralph J. "Africa and the Current World Conflict," Negro History Bulletin, IV (October, 1940), 11.

Contee, Clarence G. "Ethiopia and the Pan African Movement," Negro History Bulletin, XXXIII (May, 1970), 128.

Gregor, A. James. "Black Nationalism," Science and Society, 27 (Fall, 1963), 415-432.

Langley, Jabez Ayodele. "Garveyism and African Nationalism," Race, II (October, 1969), 157-172.

Lemarchand, Rene. "Survey of the Study of Politics in the Former Belgian Congo," American Political Science

Review, LIV (1960).

Morsell, John A.   "Black Nationalism, " Journal of Inter-
    group Relations, 3 (Winter, 1961-1962), 5-11.

Redkey, Edwin S.   "Bishop Turner's African Dream, "
    Journal of American History, 54 (September, 1967),
    271-190.

Robinson, William Russell.   "Black Nationalism American
    Style, " Duquesne University History Forum, 1970.

Roucek, Joseph.   "The Changing Relationship of the Ameri-
    can Negro to African History and Politics, " Journal
    of Human Relations, XIV (Fall, 1966), 17-26.

Simmons, Charles W.   "The Negro Intellectual's Criticism
    of Garveyism, " Negro History Bulletin, XXV (Novem-
    ber, 1961), 33.

Walden, Daniel and Kenneth Wylie.   "W. E. B. DuBois: Pan
    Africanism's Intellectual Father, " Journal of Human
    Relations, XIV (Fall, 1966), 28-41.

Weisbord, Robert G.   "The Back-to-Africa Idea, " History
    Today, 18 (January, 1968), 30-37.

Wesley, Charles H.   "International Aspects of the Negro's
    Status in the United States, " Negro History Bulletin,
    X (February, 1948), 108.

Young, Harrison.   "The Ivy League Negro Black Nationalist?"
    Harvard Crimson (September 21, 1964).

Books

Bittle, William E. and Gilbert Geis.   The Longest Way Home:
    Chief C. Sam's Back-to-Africa Movement.   Detroit:
    Wayne State University Press, 1964.

Cronon, E. D.   Black Moses: The Story of Marcus Garvey
    and the Universal Negro Improvement Association.
    Madison: University of Wisconsin Press, 1955.

Delany, M. R. and Robert Campbell.   Search for a Place:
    Black Separatism and Africa, 1860.   Ann Arbor:

University of Michigan Press, 1969.

Draper, Theodore. Black Nationalism in America. New
York: Viking, 1970.

Killian, Lewis M. The Impossible Revolution? Black Power
and the American Dream. New York: Random, 1968.

Redkey, Edwin. Black Exodus: Black Nationalists and the
Back-to-Africa Movement, 1890-1960. New Haven:
Yale University Press, 1969.

FOREIGN POLICY

Articles

Hero, Alfred O., Jr. "American Negroes and U.S. Foreign
Policy, 1937-1968," Journal of Conflict Resolutions,
13 (June, 1969), 220-251.

Johnson, Charles S. "American Policies: Race and Foreign," Negro Digest, VIII (August, 1950).

MILITARY ACTION

Articles

"The American Negro in World Wars I and II," Journal of
Negro Education, 12 (Summer, 1943), entire issue.

"Blacks and the Antiwar Movement," Liberation, 12 (November, 1967), 29-31.

Browne, Robert S. "The Freedom Movement and the War
in Vietnam," Freedomways, 5, No. 4 (Fall, 1965).

Dalfiume, Richard M. "The Fahy Committee and Desegregation of the Armed Forces," Historian, 31 (November,
1968), 1-20.

_____. "Military Segregation and the 1940 Presidential
Election," Phylon, 30 (Spring, 1969), 42-55.

Dwyer, Robert J. "The Negro in the U.S. Army,"
Sociology and Social Research, 38 (November, 1953),
103-112.

Dymally, Mervyn M. "Civil Rights and the War in Vietnam," Urban West, (October, 1967).

Fendrich, James and Michael Pearson. "Black Veterans Return," Trans-Action, 7 (March, 1970), 32-37.

Gill, Robert L. "The Post War Period and the New Negro," The Quarterly Review of Higher Education, 32 (January, 1964).

Katz, William Loren. "Six New Medal of Honor Men," Journal of Negro History, 53 (January, 1963), 77-81.

Langley, Harold D. "The Negro in the Navy and Merchant Marine, 1798-1860," Journal of Negro History, 52 (October, 1967), 273-286.

McKissick, Floyd and Whitney M. Young, Jr. "The Negro and the Army: Two Views," New Generation, 48 (Fall, 1966), 10-15.

Reddick, L. D. "The Negro Policy of the American Army Since World War II," Journal of Negro History, 38 (April, 1953), 194-215.

Stillman, Richard. "Negroes in the U.S. Armed Forces," Phylon, 30 (Summer, 1969), 139-159.

Young, Whitney M., Jr. "When the Negroes in Vietnam Come Home," Harper's, 234 (June, 1967), 63-69.

Books

Brown, Robert S. Race Relations in International Affairs. Washington, D.C.: Public Affairs Press, 1961.

Burchard, Peter. One Gallant Rush. New York: St. Martin's Press, 1965.

Silvers, John D. (ed.). The Negro in World War II. New York: Arno Press, 1968.

Stillman, Richard J. Integration of the Negro in the U.S. Armed Forces. New York: Praeger, 1968.

U.S. Department of Defense. Integration and the Negro

Officer in the Armed Forces of the United States of America. Washington, D.C., 1962.

Chapter XI

BLACKS AND URBAN POLITICS

From a political standpoint, the role of blacks in the metropolis is growing. The literature in this area is mostly very recent and much more is probably under way. Study analyses and books are being developed rapidly and the potential is great for this to become one of the fastest growing areas in the field of black politics.

There are at present no major ground-breaking studies on urban black politics, but a few historical analyses of blacks in the urban area are being used as a basis for many other works in progress.

Articles

Abrams, Charles. "The Housing Problem and the Negro," Daedalus, CXV (Winter, 1966), 64-76.

Alexander, Raymond Pace. "The Black Lawyer's Responsibility in the Urban Crisis," Negro Digest (June, 1969), 15-22.

Allen, Rosalyn. "The Impact of County and City Government Consolidation in Jacksonville Area on Black Political Power." Paper presented to State Government Class, Savannah State College, December 6, 1966.

"Cities' Outlook: Ideas Presented at Institute of Black Elected Officials," Business Week (October 4, 1969), 100.

Hatcher, R. G. "Black Role in Urban Politics," Current History, 57 (November, 1969), 287-289.

Holden, Matthew, Jr. "County Government in Ohio."

Cleveland: Cleveland Metropolitan Services Commission, 1958.

Kramer, John and Ingo Walter. "Politics in an All-Negro City," Urban Affairs Quarterly, 4 (September, 1968), 65-87.

Moody, Peter R., Jr. "The Effects of the Adoption of Metropolitan Government in Nashville and Davidson County Tennessee on Negro Political Influence." Unpublished Senior Honor Thesis, Vanderbilt University, 1965.

Patterson, Jack E. "Black Power, Municipal Style," Commonweal, 90 (August 8, 1969), 477-478.

Piven, Francis and Richard A. Cloward. "Dissensus Politics," in A. Shank (ed.), Political Power and the Urban Crisis (Boston: Holbrook Press, 1969), 243-252.

Sloan, Lee and Robert M. French. "Race and Governmental Consolidation in Jacksonville," Negro Educational Review, XXI (April-July, 1970), 72-78.

Books

Boskin, Joseph, ed. Urban Racial Violence in the Twentieth Century. Beverly Hills: Glencoe Press, 1969.

Brown, Claude. Manchild in the Promised Land. New York: Signet, 1965.

Clark, Kenneth. Dark Ghetto. New York: Harper & Row, 1967.

Drake, St. Claire and Horace Cayton. Black Metropolis. New York: Harcourt, Brace and World, 1965.

Ellis, William. White Ethics and Black Power. Chicago: Aldine, 1969.

Keil, Charles. Urban Blues. Chicago: University of Chicago Press, 1969.

McCord, William, et al. Life Styles in the Black Ghetto.

New York: W. W. Norton, 1969.

McKay, Claude. Harlem: Negro Metropolis. New York:
      E. P. Dutton, 1940.

Northwood, Lawrence K. and Ernest A. T. Barth. Urban
      Desegregation: Negro Pioneers and Their White
      Neighbors. Seattle: University of Washington Press,
      1965.

Oppenheimer, Martin. The Urban Guerrilla. New York:
      Quadrangle, 1969.

Osofsky, Gilbert. Harlem: The Making of a Ghetto, 1890-
      1930. New York: Harper and Row, 1966.

Report of the National Advisory Commission on Civil Dis-
      orders. New York: Bantam Books, 1968.

Spear, Allan H. Black Chicago, 1900-1920: The Making of
      a Negro Ghetto. New Haven: Yale University Press,
      1965.

Taeuber, Alma F. and Karl E. Negroes in Cities: Resi-
      dential Segregation and Neighborhood Change.
      Madison: University of Wisconsin Press, 1965.

Warren, Rolland W., ed. Politics and the Ghetto. New
      York: Atherton Press, 1969.

Weaver, Robert C. Dilemmas of Urban America. New
      York: Atheneum, 1965.

Chapter XII

BLACKS AND PUBLIC POLICY

Professor Robert Holmes' ground-breaking study of Black Politics and Public Policy will lead the way in this area for some time. It deals with the problems and consequence of national policy, but it also sheds some light on problems at the local level.

In general, however, this area suffers from a paucity of data, case studies and analyses of public policy statements. Professor Mack Jones' paper on "Black Office Holders in the South" in Politics '72 was an attempt to launch this type of study, but much more needs to be done. The potential impact of studies on policy makers and public policy itself is very great, for they could provide needed guidelines for the future.

Moreover, the needs and concerns of the black community, in terms of policy enactments, must be assessed and developed, and no such works have appeared to date.

EDUCATION

Articles

Delaney, Lloyd T. "The Politics of School Desegregation," Freedomways, 8, No. 4 (Fall, 1968).

Hamilton, Charles V. "Negro History: An Approach to Awareness," Negro History Bulletin, XXI (April, 1958), 168.

Holland, R. William. "School Desegregation and Community

Conflict," Western Regional School Desegregation
Projects, Title IV, June, 1971.

Howe, Florence. "Mississippi's Freedom Schools: The
Politics of Education," Harvard Educational Review
(Spring, 1965), 144-161.

Keppel, Francis. "The Emerging Partnership of Education
and Civil Rights," Journal of Negro Education, XXXIV
(Summer, 1965), 204-208.

McIntosh, William. "Some Legal and Political Problems
Involved in Desegregation and Integration in the Public
Schools, with Special Emphasis on Louisiana,"
Quarterly Review of Higher Education Among Negroes,
23 (October, 1955), 140-152.

Mahan, Thomas W. "The Busing of Students for Equal Op-
portunities," Journal of Negro Education, XXXVII
(Summer, 1968), 291-300.

Smith, Benjamin F. "Public School Integration: An Annotated Bibliography," Negro Educational Review, VII
(April, 1956), 60-78.

_____. "Racial Integration in Public Education: An An-
notated Bibliography, Part V," Negro Educational Review, XIV (January, 1963), 5-7.

Wolman, H. L. and Norman Thomas. "Black Interest,
Black Groups and Black Influence in the Federal
Process: The Cases of Housing and Education,"
Journal of Politics, 32, No. 4 (November, 1970),
501-522.

Books

Ashmore, Harry S. The Negro and the Schools. rev. ed.
Chapel Hill: University of North Carolina Press,
1954.

Barrett, Russell H. Honorary Nigger: Integration at Ole
Miss. New York: Quadrangle Books.

Bond, Horace Mann. The Education of the Negro in the
American Social Order. New York: Octagon Books,
1966.

Brown, Hugh Victor. A History of the Education of Negroes
    in North Carolina. Raleigh: Irving Swain Press,
    1961.

Bullock, Henry Allen. A History of Negro Education in the
    South, from 1619 to the Present. Cambridge,
    Massachusetts: Harvard University Press, 1967.

Caldwell, Dista H. The Education of the Negro Child. New
    York: Carleton Press, 1961.

Clift, Virgil A. Negro Education in America; Its Adequacy,
    Problems and Needs. New York: Harper and
    Brothers, 1962.

Dissertations

Badger, William V. A Systematic Analysis of the U.S.
    Supreme Court Cases Dealing with Education: 1790-
    1951. Florida State University, 1953.

Dauterive, Verna B. Historical Legal Development of Inte-
    gration in Public Schools. University of Southern
    California, 1966.

Hearn, Edell M. Public Educational Changes Through Legis-
    lation in Tennessee 1935-1959. University of Tennes-
    see, 1959.

Rice, Pamela H. Racial Discrimination in Education Under
    the United States Constitution. University of Wis-
    consin, 1953.

Saunders, Socrates W. Legal Aspects of the Education of
    Negroes with Special Emphasis on the Equalization
    Principle. University of Pittsburgh, 1943.

120

WELFARE

Articles

Cloward, Richard A. and Richard M. Elman. "The First
Congress of the Poor," The Nation, 202 (February 7,
1966), 148-151.

Ladd, Everett C., Jr. "The Negro's Priorities: Welfare
or Status," The Nation, 199 (October 19, 1964), 243-
246.

ECONOMIC PROGRAMS

Articles and Dissertations

DeLeon, James Maurice III. "Power Struggle--The Fight of
the Black Man to Gain Economic Control of His Community," The Third World Journal.

Form, W. H. and Joan Huber. "Income, Race and the
Ideology of Political Efficacy," Journal of Politics,
35, No. 3 (August, 1971), 480-497.

Petrof, John V. "The Effect of Student Boycotts Upon the
Purchasing Habits of Negro Families in Atlanta,
Georgia," Negro Educational Review, XIII (July-
October, 1962), 114-119.

Williams, William J. "Attacking Poverty in the Watts
Area: Small Business Development Under the Economic Opportunity Act of 1964." Doctoral dissertation, University of Southern California, 1966.

Books

Humphrey, Hubert H. War on Poverty. New York:
McGraw-Hill Book Company, 1964.

Chapter XIII

BLACKS AND THE SUPREME COURT--
BLACK JUDGES

The literature on the Supreme Court and blacks is vast. The legalistic approach of black pressure groups helped to produce this data. Moreover, the legalistic orientation of the political system and its constitutional basis have given rise to this facet of political strategy.

The Supreme Court has come to be seen as the chief protector and advancer of black rights. Moreover, it has been the least susceptible to political pressures and the governmental institution most responsive to black demands. A black judge lays the story bare in his rather comprehensive study of the court in The Petitioner. He cites the Supreme Court's support on various occasions of segregation, state's rights and property rights, to the disadvantages of black Americans, but nevertheless finds the Court's record in equality advancement to be commendable.

In reviewing The Petitioner, Professor Samuel Cook notes that the Court has not always fought racism in the American system. In fact, it has often justified and sanctified racism, and thus does not merit the total allegiance of black Americans. [Samuel Cook, Review of The Petitioners by Loren Miller, Journal of Negro History (July, 1966).]

This dilemma has characterized most of the literature on the Court, which is a medley of praise and criticism. Some works offer apologies, others unreservedly uphold and approve.

The range of the literature covers all areas of black rights, from voting rights to public accommodations and housing. Despite the generally good coverage, more works on black judges and their role, and on their particular brand of jurisprudence are still needed.

Professor Lois Moreland, of Spelman College, wrote a pioneering study in 1969 entitled Racism and the Law. It explores the intricate racist character of the law itself and views law as a barrier to equality and justice. Moreland's book will hopefully lead to further exploration in this area of black politics.

BLACKS AND THE SUPREME COURT

Articles

Alexander, Raymond P. "The Upgrading of the Negro States by Supreme Court Decisions," The Journal of Negro History, XXX (April, 1945), 117-149.

Alilunas, Lee. "Legal Restrictions on the Negro in Politics," Journal of Negro History, XXV (April, 1940), 153-202.

Barker, Lucius J. "Third Parties in Litigation: A Systemic View of the Judicial Function," Journal of Politics (February, 1967).

"Barrier Falls: The U.S. Negro Moves to Vote; Voting Rights Act of 1965," Newsweek, 66 (August 16, 1965), 15-16.

Beech, Gould. "The State of Civil Liberties Today," New Republic, 117 (August 11, 1947), 10.

Bernstein, Barton J. "Case Law in Pleasy vs. Ferguson," Journal of Negro History, XLVIII, No. 3 (July, 1962).

Blivin, Bruce. "Law Against Discrimination," New Republic, 119 (September 6, 1948), 11.

Boyd, W. M. "Negroes and Governmental Services: An

Appraisal," Quarterly Review of Higher Education Among Negroes, XIV (April, 1946), 44-54.

Browne, Vincent J. "The Elimination of Segregation by Executive Orders and Federal Administration Policies," Journal of Negro Education, XX (Summer, 1961), 450-459.

Carter, Elmer A. "The Negro in Courts," Opportunity, X (April, 1933).

Chick, C. A. "Some Recent United States Supreme Court Decisions Affecting the Rights of Negro Workers," Journal of Negro Education, XVI (Spring, 1947), 172-179.

"Civil Rights and the Warren Court," Ebony, XXV, No. 4, (February, 1970), 27-34.

Claude, Richard. "Constitutional Voting Rights and Early U.S. Supreme Court Doctrine," Journal of Negro History, 51 (April, 1966), 114-124.

Corwin, E. S. "The Dred Scott Decision in the Light of Contemporary Legal Doctrines," American Historical Review, XVII (October, 1911), 52-69.

Davis, John and Cornelius L. Golightly. "Negro Employment in the Federal Government," Phylon, VI (Fall, 1946), 337.

Dickerson, Earl B. "Negro Rights and the Supreme Court," The Nation, 175 (July 12, 1952), 26-38.

Dixon, R. G. "Civil Rights in Transportation and the I.C.C.," George Washington Law Review (October, 1962), 198-241.

Douglass, Paul H. "Trends and Developments: The 1960 Voting Rights Bill: The Struggle, the Final Results and the Reason," Journal of Intergroup Relations, 1, No. 3 (1960), 82-86.

Ehrlich, Walter. "Was the Dred Scott Case Valid?" Journal of American History, LV (September, 1968).

Fagget, H. L. "The Negroes Who Do Not Want to End

Segregation," Quarterly Review of Higher Education Among Negroes, XXIII (July, 1955), 120-121.

Feinstein, Isidor. "The Supreme Court and Civil Liberties," The Nation, 144 (February 6, 1937), 151-153.

Fleming, Harold C. "The Federal Executive and Civil Rights, 1961-1965," in Talcott Parson and Kenneth Clark (eds.), The Negro American (Boston: Houghton Mifflin, 1966), 371-400.

Gill, Robert L. "The Civil Rights Act, 1964: The Promise and Fulfillment of American Democracy," Quarterly Review of Higher Education Among Negroes, XXXII (April, 1964), 51-67.

_____. "Civil Rights Legislation, 1865-1965: The Beacon of Ordered Liberty," Quarterly Review of Higher Education Among Negroes, XXXIII (April, 1965), 79-93.

_____. "Defender of Civil Liberties," Quarterly Review of Higher Education Among Negroes, XVII (January, 1949), 1-9.

_____. "The Negro before the Supreme Court, 1968," Quarterly Review of Higher Education Among Negroes, 37 (July, 1969), 122-135.

_____. "The Negro in the Supreme Court," Negro History Bulletin, XXVIII (December, 1964), 51.

_____. "The Negro in the Supreme Court, 1940," Quarterly Review of Higher Education Among Negroes, XXXIII (October, 1965), 205-212.

_____. "The Negro in the Supreme Court, 1954-1964," Quarterly Review of Higher Education Among Negroes, XXXIII (January, 1965), 1-19.

_____. "The Negro in the Supreme Court, 1961," Negro Educational Review, XIII (April, 1962), 60-75.

_____. "The Negro in the Supreme Court, 1962," Negro Educational Review, XIV (July-October, 1963), 101-125.

_____. "The Negro Standing Before the Supreme Court

1865," Quarterly Review of Higher Education Among Negroes, XXXIII (July, 1965), 161-173.

_____. "The Role of Five Negro Lawyers in the Civil Rights Struggle," Quarterly Review of Higher Education Among Negroes, XXXI (April, 1962), 31-58.

_____. "The School Segregation Cases and State Reactions," Quarterly Review of Higher Education Among Negroes (October, 1956), 163-169.

_____. "The Shaping of Race Relations by the Federal Judiciary in Court Decisions," Negro Educational Review, XI (January, 1960), 15-23.

_____. "Smith vs. Allwright and Reactions in Some of the Southern States," Quarterly Review of Higher Education Among Negroes, XV (July, 1967), 154-169.

_____. "The Supreme Court, 1963," Quarterly Review of Higher Education Among Negroes, (October, 1964), 159-176.

Hartman, Paul. "Civil Rights and Minorities," New Republic, 122 (January 30, 1950), 20.

Hast, Adele. "The Legal Status of the Negro in Virginia, 1705-1765," Journal of Negro History, LIV, No. 3 (July, 1969).

Havens, Charles W., III. "Federal Legislation to Safeguard Voting Rights: the Civil Rights Act of 1960," Virginia Law Review, 46 (1960), 945-975.

Herbster, Ben M. "FCC Ban Eyed in Mississippi," New York Times (December 31, 1969), 18.

Heyman, Ira M. "Federal Remedies for Voteless Negroes," California Law Review, 48 (1960), 190-215.

Hollis, E. V. "Supreme Court Decision on Segregation," Vital Speeches, 21 (November 1, 1954), 823-826.

Hope, John, II and Edward E. Shelton. "The Negro in the Federal Government," Journal of Negro Education (Fall, 1963), 367-374.

Horsky, C. A. "The Supreme Court, Congress and the Right

to Vote," Ohio State Law Journal, 20 (Summer, 1959), 549-556.

Imes, William Lloyd. "The Legal Status of Free Negroes and Slaves in Tennessee," Journal of Negro History, IV, No. 3 (July, 1919).

Kaiser, Ernest. "The Federal Government and the Negro," Science and Society, XX (Winter, 1956).

Konvitz, Milton B. "A Nation Within a Nation, The Negro and the Supreme Court," The American Scholar, XI (Winter, 1941-1942), 67-78.

Lemmon, Sarah M. "Transportation Segregation in the Federal Courts, Since 1865," Journal of Negro History (April, 1963).

Lloyd, Raymond Gram. "The States Rights Myth and Southern Oppositions to Federal Anti-Lynching Legislation," Negro Educational Review, V (Fall, 1950), 1950), 78-88.

Lynch, John R. "The Civil Rights Bill," Journal of Negro History, XII (October, 1927), 667-669.

Lytle, Clifford M. "The History of the Civil Rights Bill, 1965," Journal of Negro History, LI (October, 1966), 275-287.

McCarthy, L. Thorne and Russell B. Stevenson. "Voting Rights Act of 1965: An Evaluation," Harvard Civil Rights Law Review, 3 (Spring, 1968), 357-411.

McGill, R. "Civil Rights for the Negroes," Atlantic Monthly, 184 (November, 1949), 64-66.

McKinney, Theophiles E., Jr. "United States Transportation Segregation," Quarterly Review of Higher Education Among Negroes, XXII (July, 1954), 101-148.

_____. "U.S. Supreme Court Decision of May 17, 1954, Editorial Comment," Quarterly Review of Higher Education Among Negroes, XII (July, 1954), 49.

Marshall, Thurgood. "An Evaluation of Recent Efforts to Achieve Racial Integration Through Resort to the

Courts," Journal of Negro Education, XX (Summer, 1952).

Miller, Loren. "How Supreme Court Overcame Its Racism," Ebony, XXI, No. 5 (March, 1966).

Motley, Constance Baker. "The Legal Status of the Negro in the United States," in John P. Davis (ed.), The American Negro Reference Book (New Jersey: Prentice-Hall, 1966), 484-521.

Murphy, L. E. "The Civil Rights Laws of 1875," Journal of Negro History, XIII (April, 1927), 110-127.

Nelson, Bernard. "The Negro Before the Supreme Court," Phylon, VIII (First Quarter, 1947), 34-48.

Pentecoste, Joseph. "The New Black Television--a White Strategy: A Commentary," Inner City Issues (October, 1969), 4-11.

Peterson, Gladys. "The Present Status of the Negro Separate School as Defined by Court Decisions," Journal of Negro Education, IV (Winter, 1935), 351-374.

Preston, E. Delorus. "The Negro and the Bill of Rights," Quarterly Review of Higher Education Among Negroes, X (April, 1942), 86-88.

"The Right to Vote," New Republic, 162 (January 3, 1970), 8-9.

"Supreme Court and Negro Suffrage," The World Work, 6 (June, 1903), 3491-3492.

Taylor, Joseph H. "The Fourteenth Amendment, the Negro and the Spirit of the Times," Journal of Negro History, XLV (January, 1960), 21-37.

Thompson, Daniel C. "The Role of the Federal Courts in the Changing Status of Negroes Since World War II," Journal of Negro Education, XXX (Spring, 1961), 94-101.

Tinsley, James A. "Roosevelt, Foraker, Brownsville Affairs," Journal of Negro History, XL (January, 1956), 43-65.

Trent, W. "Federal Sanctions Directed Against Racial

Discrimination," Phylon, 111 (Second Quarter, 1952), 171-182.

Turner, Albert L. "Negro and the Supreme Court," Quarterly Review of Higher Education Among Negroes, 4 (April, 1936), 75-78.

"Tuskegee Case and the Political Question Dilemma," Georgia Bar Journal, 23 (May, 1961), 545-548.

Ulmer, Sidney S. "Earl Warren and the Brown Decision," Journal of Politics, 33, No. 3 (August, 1971), 285-297.

_____. "Supreme Court Behavior in Racial Exclusion Cases: 1935-1960," American Political Science Review, LVI (June, 1962), 325-330.

"Voting in the South; Supreme Court Decision Fails to Let Negroes into the Polls," Life, 16 (May 15, 1944), 32-34.

Waite, Edward F. "The Negro in the Supreme Court," Minnesota Law Review, 30, No. 4 (March, 1946), 219-314.

White, W. "Negro and the Supreme Court," Harper's Magazine, 162 (January, 1931), 238-246.

Williamson, Hugh. "The Role of the Courts in the Status of the Negro," Journal of Negro History, XL (January, 1955).

Wright, Benjamin F. "The Rights of Majorities and of Minorities in the 1961 Term of the Supreme Court," American Political Science Review, LVII (March, 1963), 98-115.

Dissertations

Anderson, Robert L. Negro Suffrage in Relation to American Federalism, 1957-63. University of Florida, 1964.

Hamilton, Charles V. Southern Federal Courts and the Right of Negroes to Vote, 1957-1962. University of Chicago, 1964.

Jans, Ralph T. Negro Civil Rights and the Supreme Court,
     1865-1949. University of Chicago, 1951.

McGuinn, Henry J. The Courts and the Changing Status of
     Negroes in Maryland. Columbia University, 1940.

Books

Bennett, Lerone. Black Power, U.S.A. Chicago: Johnson
     Publishing Company, 1968.

Berger, Monroe. Equality by Statute. New York: Anchor
     Books, 1968.

Blaustein, Albert P. and Robert Zangrando. Civil Rights
     and the American Negro. New York: Washington
     Square Press, 1968.

Catterall, Helen, ed. Judicial Cases Concerning American
     Slavery and the Negro. Washington, D.C., 1926.

Friedman, Leon, ed. Southern Justice. Cleveland: Meridi-
     an Books, 1967.

Kalven, Harry J. The Negro and the First Amendment.
     Columbus, Ohio: Ohio State University Press, 1965.

McKissick, Floyd. Three-Fifths of a Man. New York:
     Macmillan, 1969.

Miller, Loren. The Petitioners: The Story of the Supreme
     Court of the United States and the Negro. New York:
     Pantheon Books, 1966.

Nelson, Bernard H. The Fourteenth Amendment and the
     Negro Since 1920. Washington, D.C.: Catholic
     University Press.

Strong, Donald S. Negroes, Ballots and Judges: National
     Voting Rights Legislation in the Federal Courts.
     University: University of Alabama Press, 1968.

Taper, Bernard. Gomillion versus Lightfoot: The Tuskegee
     Gerrymander Case. New York: McGraw-Hill, 1962.

Tenbrock, J. Equal Under the Law. New York: Collier

Books, 1965.

Tussman, Joseph, ed. The Supreme Court on Racial Dis-
    crimination. New York: Oxford University Press,
    1967.

Vose, Clement E. Caucasians Only: The Supreme Court,
    the NAACP and the Restrictive Covenant Cases.
    Berkeley: University of California Press, 1959.

BLACK JUDGES

Articles

Bennett, Lerone. "Lawyer Who Turned Down a Judgeship,"
    Ebony, XVI, No. 4 (February, 1961), 25-32.

Black Law Journal Interview. "George W. Crockett: The
    Opener," The Black Law Journal, 1, No. 3 (Winter,
    1971), 247-259.

Chaplain, Marvin. "Virginia's Black Justice," New Repub-
    lic, 124 (January 29, 1951), 17.

Cook, Beverly Blair. "Black Representation in the Third
    Branch," The Black Law Journal, 1, No. 3 (Winter,
    1971), 260-279.

"Fourth Negro Candidate for Municipal Judge, Philadelphia,"
    New Republic, 137 (September 9, 1957), 6.

"Judge Branch of Greene County," Ebony, XXVI, No. 10
    August 1971) 82-85.

"Negro Judges," Ebony, XI, No. 4 (February, 1956), 61-
    65.

"Negro Judgeships at Record High," Ebony, XVII, No. 9
    (July, 1962), 79.

Roy, Jessie H. "Colored Judges," Negro History Bulletin,
    28 (March-April, 1965), 135-137, 158.

_____. "Negro Judges in the United States," Negro
    History Bulletin, 28 (February, 1965), 108-111.

Sanders, C. L. "Detroit's Rebel Judge Crocket,"

Ebony, 24 (August, 1969), 114-116.

Smith, Warner. "Loren Miller: Advocate for Blacks,"
The Black Law Journal, 1, No. 1 (Spring, 1971), 6-
15.

"Supreme Court Justice Thurgood Marshall," Negro History
Bulletin, 30 (October, 1967), 4-5.

Washington, Michelle. "Black Judges in White America,"
The Black Law Journal, 1, No. 3 (Winter, 1971),
241-245.

_____. "Constance Baker Motley: Black Woman, Black
Judge," The Black Law Journal, 1, No. 2 (Summer,
1971), 173-179.

APPENDIX I

This appendix lists all of the major articles in the New York Times covering the Black Republicans (dubbed the Black and Tan Republicans) in the South from 1900 to 1956. Coverage of the small organization by other sources is almost non-existent; the Times is the only major source. The articles in this section have been arranged in chronological order, and should be helpful to researchers in this phase of Black political history.

BLACK AND TAN REPUBLICANS

BIBLIOGRAPHY

1900

"South Carolina Convention Republicans Elect Two Whites and Two Negroes," March 21, 1900, p. 7.

"Hot Fight in Tennessee," April 21, 1900, p. 1.

"Split in Republican Ranks," April 21, 1900, p. 1.

"Many Republican Contests," May 28, 1900, p. 2.

"Mississippi Bolters Convention," June 11, 1900, p. 2.

"The Republican Convention," June 14, 1900, p. 1.

"National Republican Committee Meets," June 14, 1900, p. 1.

"Republican Committee Settles Contests," June 15, 1900, p. 1.

"Sentiment of the State Delegation," June 18, 1900, p. 1.

"New National Committee," June 20, 1900, p. 1.

"North Carolina Convention," May 3, 1900, p. 3.

"Notice of Contest of Thirty Delegates Received...,"
    May 28, 1900, pp. 2-5.

"Mississippi Compromise," June 5, 1900, p. 2.

"Philadelphia Meeting: Contests for Membership in the Convention Considered and Settled," June 14, 1900, p. 1-2.

"Warmouth Faction Wins Louisiana Case," June 15, 1900, p. 15.

"Republicans Gather for Convention," June 13, 1900, p. 1.

"Georgia Delegates Named," March 9, 1900, p. 14.

"Kentucky Republicans Meet--State Convention Passes Resolution Endorsing the President--Election Law Denounced," April 2, 1900, p. 1.

"Alabama Sends Two Delegates," April 20, 1900, p. 3.

"First Draft of Republican Platform," June 18, 1900, p. 1.

"Representation of the South in Congress, January 19, 1900, p. 6.

"South Carolina Republicans Will Contest for Delegates," February 6, 1900, p. 3.

"National Convention Platform: Tariff Plank Dilemma," February 27, 1900, 6:2.

"National Afro-American Council to Present Questions of Lynching and Civil Rights," June 18, 1900, p. 18.

"Ruling Against Alabama Delegates," June 14, 1900, p. 1-2.

"Suffrage Plan," January 19, 1900, p. 6.

"Republican Committee--Temporary Officers at Convention Selected," June 17, 1900, p. 3.

"First Session of Convention," June 20, 1900, p. 2.

"How the States Stand," June 20, 1900, p. 2.

"Southern Delegates Protest," June 21, 1900, p. 2.

"Reports of Committees," June 21, 1900, p. 2.

"Gavel for Chairman," June 21, 1900, p. 2.

"For Reduced Representation," June 22, 1900, p. 2.

"E. H. R. Green Turned Down," June 22, 1900, p. 2.

"Mr. Payne Introduces a Resolution--Ruling Against Alabama Delegates," June 14, 1900, p. 1.

"Hanna Pleads for Unity of Action," June 16, 1900, p. 2.

1904

"Few Delegation Contests (Notices of Eight Only Filed with Republican National Committee)," April 30, 1904, p. 3.

"W. L. Saunders, "Decision Deprives Hughes of 16 Votes (Contesting Georgia Delegation Seated by Committee)," June 1, 1904, p. 2.

"The Negro in the Platform," June 29, 1904, p. 6.

"Republicans to Uphold the Party in the South," December 24, 1904, p. 5.

"Candidates and Campaign," June 23, 1904, p. 8.

"Democratic States in Republican Convention," June 24, 1904, p. 5.

"Lily Whites Keep Up Fight," June 21, 1904, p. 2.

"LaFollette Men," June 22, 1904, p. 2.

"Georgia Fights Cause Delay--Several Black Delegates Favoring Hughes Win Contest," June 2, 1904, p. 4-5.

1908

"More Taft Delegates--But a Kentucky District May Be Contested by Fairbanks Men," May 6, 1908, p. 3.

"Alabama for Taft--Thompson Wing of Party Instructs its Delegates for Secretary," May 7, 1908, p. 3.

"Taft Wins in Kentucky--Fairbanks' Men are Beaten and Delegates Instructed for Secretary," May 8, 1908, p. 3.

"Stampede to Taft to Block Roosevelt--Utah and Texas Demands for President Have Frightened the Leaders," May 12, 1908, p. 2.

"Louisiana for Taft--Negro Among the Delegates Chosen at State Convention," May 8, 1908, p. 2.

"24 Seats Won by Taft Men--National Committee Seats Administration Delegates in Alabama and Arkansas--Anti-Taft Men Protest--Objection to Hitchcock and His Assistants Sitting on Committee Voted Down," June 6, 1908, p. 1.

"May Form a Negro Party--Action by Republican Committee Reseated by Southern Delegation," June 7, 1908, p. 2.

"Negroes Bitter, Says Dick," June 10, 1908, p. 2.

"President Approves Agreement," June 10, 1908, p. 2.

"McHarg Stirs the Committee," June 10, 1908, p. 3.

"Taft Men Invade an Anti-South Plan--Fear Both Would Follow Attempt to Reduce Delegates--Thirty-four More Votes for Taft--Missouri Hughes Delegates, Sidetracked are Indignant--Negro Delegates from North Carolina Excluded," June 11, 1908, p. 1.

"Taft Gains Fifty Votes--Hatchet Displayed in the Hall--Oliver Tennessee Contest," June 12, 1908, p. 4.

"Tennessee Contests," June 12, 1908, p. 4.

"Lyon Faction is Seated," June 12, 1908, p. 4.

"Committee Decides the Final Contests," June 13, 1908, p. 2.

"Louisiana Delegates to Fight," June 13, 1908, p. 2.

"Call for White Men Only," June 13, 1908, p. 2.

"Negro Question in Virginia," June 13, 1908, p. 2.

"Want to Reduce Delegates--Allies to Offer Resolution Cutting Down Southern Representation," June 14, 1908, p. 3.

"Want to Name Roosevelt--Georgia and West Virginia Delegation to Plan Campaign," June 15, 1908, p. 2.

"Organization of the Delegation," June 16, 1908, p. 3.

"Many States Organized," June 16, 1908, p. 3.

"Southern Men Non-Committed," June 16, 1908, p. 3.

"South May Lose Delegates--Rule Committee Refuses to Vote Down Proposal for New Rule," June 17, 1908, p. 2.

"110 Seats Contested," June 17, 1908, p. 2.

"Reference to their Rights Rouses Delegates--Move to Cut Representation of the South," June 17, 1908, p. 3.

"To End Power of the South," June 18, 1908, p. 3.

"Ohio Saves Delegates in the South," June 18, 1908, p. 1.

"Convention's Second Day--Roosevelt Outburst Followed by a Fight Over Southern Delegation," June 18, 1908, p. 2.

"Astute Arrangements Made in the South," June 21, 1908, pt. 5, p. 1.

"34 for Taft, One for Foraker," June 11, 1908, p. 2.

"Political Booms Started in Chicago--Taft's Brother Announces that He Expects the Secretary to Be Nominated on First Ballot," June 5, 1908, p. 2.

"Allies Admit Taft Will Win--Delegation from Florida Divided, but Taft Men Will Be Seated in All the Other Cases," June 10, 1908, p. 1.

"More Taft Men Seated--Compromise in Louisiana is Permitted by the President," June 10, 1908, p. 2.

"South Made Solid for Taft," June 18, 1908, p. 1.

"Committee Has Yet to Consider Contest Involving Ninety-four Votes," June 11, 1908, p. 2.

"Committee Decides the Final Contests; Anti-Taft Men from Virginia Seated Because of a Call for White Men Only," June 13, 1908, p. 2.

"The Colored Delegates," June 19, 1908, p. 12.

1912

"Roosevelt Fight on to Grab Committee," June 3, 1912, p. 3.

"Taft Advises Open Contest Hearings," June 3, 1912, p. 1.

"Taft Wins in First Contest," June 8, 1912, pp. 1-2.

"Division of Delegates," June 8, 1912, p. 2.

"President Wins the Georgia and Florida Contests," June 9, 1912, p. 2.

"Louisiana Case Taken Up," June 12, 1912, p. 2.

"Negroes Speak for Taft," June 14, 1912, p. 2.

"Plan Delegation Changes," June 14, 1912, p. 2.

"Rival Taft Delegates," June 5, 1912, p. 3.

"Mix-Up in Tennessee," June 5, 1912, p. 3.

"Negro Delegates Accuse Taft Men," June 15, 1912, p. 3.

"Did Send $1000 to Negro Delegate," June 16, 1912, p. 4.

"Contest Bitterly Fought to the End," June 16, 1912, p. 5.

"Ten Southern Delegates and Woodruff and March of New York Shift," June 17, 1912, p. 1.

"To Open Fire on Root," June 17, 1912, p. 2.

"Most of Bolters Negroes," June 17, 1912, p. 2.

"Taft Men Say They'll Win Today and that Col. Roosevelt Will Bolt; Negroes Tell Bribes to Beat Taft," June 18, 1912, p. 1.

"Row in Georgia Caucus," June 18, 1912, p. 2.

"Bolters Back in Taft Camp; Misled by Roosevelt Managers, Georgia Negroes Declare," June 18, 1912, p. 2.

"Faith in Negro Delegates," June 19, 1912, p. 3.

"Bolt Starts in Credentials Committee and Roosevelt Men All Walk Out; Plan Now for Third Party," June 20, 1912, p. 1.

"Roosevelt Plan Third Party: To Name Full Ticket in States He Controls and Split Solid South," June 20, 1912, p. 1.

"Bolters Voting on Contests," June 21, 1912, p. 1.

"Delegates Come to Blow," June 23, 1912, p. 1.

"Roosevelt Men in Uproar," June 23, 1912, p. 2.

"Roosevelt Men to Fight Harder--Threaten to Carry Contest to Delegates to Convention Floor," June 10, 1912.

"More Negroes Tell of Bribe Offers," June 18, 1912, p. 1.

"After Negro Delegates: Booker T. Washington Said to be Working for Roosevelt," May 5, 1912, p. 6.

1916

"Leaders Say it Will be Hughes or Roosevelt: Sent a Negro Contestant," June 2, 1916, pp. 1-2.

"Decision Deprives Hughes of 16 Votes: Contesting Georgia Delegates Seated by Committee," June 2, 1916, p. 2.

"Georgia Fight Causes Delay--Several Blun Delegates Favoring Hughes Win Contest," June 2, 1916, p. 2.

"Few Delegation Contest (Notices of Eight Only Filed with Republican National Committee)," April 30, 1916, p. 3.

"Fails to Instruct in Alabama," May 21, 1916, p. 3.

W. L. Saunders, "Decision Deprives Hughes of 16 Votes (Contesting Georgia Delegation Seated by Committee) First Day's Work on Hearings," June 1, 1916, p. 2.

"Party Split in Georgia," April 13, 1916, p. 6.

"Contesting Georgia Delegation Seated by Committee," June 1, 1916, p. 2.

"Negro Delegates Scarce," June 5, 1916, p. 4.

"Southern Delegation," June 7, 1916, p. 1.

"Apportionment is Approved," June 8, 1916, p. 2.

"Vian Won't Give Up," June 14, 1916, p. 3.

1920

"South Carolina Republicans Will Contest for Convention Seats," February 5, 1920, p. 1.

"Mild Republican Stand by Lenroot Reservation--Others Join Stand Pat Group," February 15, 1920, p. 1.

"Negro Republicans Bolt in Three States," April 29, 1920, p. 2.

"Contest One-Eighth of Votes at Chicago," May 21, 1920, p. 2.

"122 Contests Before National Committee," May 29, 1920, p. 17.

"Lowden Men Gain in First Contests," June 1, 1920, p. 1.

"Queer Southern Republicans," June 1, 1920, p. 14.

"Aims Hard Blows at Lily Whites," June 4, 1920, p. 1.

"Assails Lily Whites Policy," June 6, 1920, p. 18.

"Move to Decrease Southern Delegates," June 14, 1920, p. 3.

"Alexander Carlisle Seeks Republican Convention Seat," June 7, 1920, p. 1.

"Republican Big '4' is Bennett's Goul," February 9, 1920, p. 15.

"All Lynching a Crime, Hays Tells Negroes," February 11, 1920, p. 3.

"Republican Workers Declare Wood and Johnson Will Dominate National Convention," March 29, 1920, p. 17.

"H. L. Johnson Declares Negroes are Lynched in Georgia for Voting Republican Ticket," July 9, 1920, p. 3.

"Anti-Suffragists Again Fight Hayes," February 8, 1920, p. 1.

"Anna S. Banks, Negress, is Regular Accredited Member of Clarke County Delegation," March 4, 1920, p. 7.

"Louisiana 'Black and Tan' Faction Contests Mrs. Herberts Right to Seat," May 31, 1920, p. 2.

"Republicans Look to South for 1924," December 12, 1920, p. 20.

"Georgia Fight Taken Up," June 2, 1920, p. 2.

"Governor Gains in South," June 6, 1920, p. 1-2.

"Two Virginians Out for Vice-Presidency," June 6, 1920, p. 7.

"North Carolina to Present Pritchard for Vice-Presidency," June 7, 1920, p. 1.

"Lowden Holds Southern Votes," June 9, 1920, p. 1.

"Georgia Faction May Contest Johnson's Election to National Committee," June 11, 1920, p. 1.

"Johnson Wins Georgia Fight," June 11, 1920, p. 2.

"Governor Morrow Makes a Hit," June 14, 1920, p. 3.

"Mississippi State Convention Fight on Delegates to National Convention," April 6, 1920, p. 17.

"Contest of Votes--Many Filed," May 21, 1920, p. 17.

"Black and Tan Faction Contests Right of Mrs. C. S. Herbert to Seat," May 11, 1920, p. 2.

"Local Convention in Places Having Negroes are Banned," June 6, 1920, p. 1.

"Sub-Committee Appointed to Report on Representation from the South," June 6, 1920, p. 1.

"National Convention Passes Resolution to End Repetition of Scandals in the South," June 14, 1920.

"Arkansas Convention. Negro Delegates Denied Seats, Name Separate Ticket," April 29, 1920, p. 2.

"The Two Conventions," May 30, 1920, p. 2.

"Local Conventions in Places Barring Negroes," June 4, 1920, p. 14.

"Contest of Votes," June 1, 1920, p. 14.

1924

"Sen. Johnson Attacks--Restoration of Southern Representation was Increased to Aid Him," January 20, 1924, pt. 20, p. 1.

"Carry Fight to Cleveland," June 2, 1924, p. 1.

"Negro Delegates: Rival Republican Delegates from Georgia to Go Convention," June 2, 1924, p. 1.

"Sen. Johnson Attacks Restoration of Southern Representation," June 4, 1924, p. 3.

"Johnson Negro Delegation Seated Following Production of Letter Written by President Harding to G. B. Stemp," June 5, 1924, p. 2.

"Contests Among Delegation Fears that Question of Representation May be Opened," June 6, 1924, p. 3.

"Contest May Be Carried To Convention," June 6, 1924, p. 3.

"Fight Between Two Negro Delegations," June 6, 1924, p. 3.

"Republicans Face Fight on the South," June 6, 1924, p. 3.

"Hope for Southern States," June 6, 1924, p. 14.

"Decision to Seat 'Black and Tans' from Tennessee," June 8, 1924, p. 2.

"Warmoth Protest Against Seating of Delegates," June 8, 1924, p. 2.

"Georgia Harmony Restored," July 16, 1924, p. 3.

"Letter to the Editor on Southern Representation," January 1, 1924, p. 22.

"Senator Johnson Attacks Restoration of Southern Representation," January 4, 1924, p. 3.

"Coolidge's Managers Deny that Southern Representation Was Increased to Aid Him," January 20, 1924, p. 5.

"Brandy Elected Delegate from Virginia," February 1, 1924, p. 19.

"Kentucky Delegation to National Convention Told to Vote for Coolidge," February 13, 1924, p. 1.

"Meyer Tells of Intention to Import Negroes on Primary Day," March 15, 1924, p. 15.

"Mississippi Delegations Instructed to Vote for Coolidge," March 26, 1924, p. 1.

"Georgia Rival Delegates Go to Cleveland to Contest Seats at Republican National Convention," June 2, 1924, p. 1.

"Contest May Be Carried to Convention," June 6, 1924, p. 3.

"National Convention of 1924 Sidelights on Radio," July 6, 1924, p. 13.

"Texas--Ku Klux Klan Denounced at State Conventions," August 14, 1924, p. 2.

"South--Letter from Mrs. A. C. Darling," November 21, 1924, p. 18.

"Johnson Delegates from Georgia are Seated by National
   Committee," June 5, 1924, p. 2.

"Warmoth Opposes South Delegates," June 8, 1924, p. 2.

"Hopes Southern Black Will Name Candidate," September 14,
   1924, p. 30.

"Negro Delegates Rival Republicans Delegates from Georgia,
   Go to Convention," June 2, 1924, p. 1.

"Louisiana Delegates Don't Represent the State," June 8,
   1924, p. 2.

"Negroes Want Plank to Denounce Klan," June 9, 1924,
   p. 2.

"M. Kellan Assails Republican Planks" June 13, 1924,
   p. 6.

"National Convention of 1924 Three Delegates on Radio,"
   July 6, 1924, p. 13.

"Southern States Among Delegation Fear that Question of
   Representation May Be Reopened," June 6, 1924, p.
   3.

1928

"Contests Over Georgia and Wisconsin Members Develops
   at National Convention," June 16, 1928, p. 2.

"Mississippi Bar Election from Negroes to Nominate Delegates for National Republican Convention," March 12,
   1928, p. 2.

"State Convention Split Over National Policies Matters,"
   May 23, 1928, p. 2.

"Republican Party--National Convention Delegates Alternates
   and Visitors," June 3, 1928, p. 1.

"Southern Republicans," November 20, 1928, p. 30.

"Negro Leaders Restrained from Holding Company," March
   12, 1928, p. 2.

"The Delegation Contests," June 4, 1928, p. 4.

"Two More From Kentucky," June 5, 1928, p. 1.

"Perry Howard's Anti-Lily White Faction Recognized," June 6, 1928, p. 1.

"Four Georgians Seated," June 7, 1928, p. 1.

"Wurzback Opens Attack," June 7, 1928, p. 3.

"Four Lowden Men Seated," June 7, 1928, p. 3.

"Tennessee Fight Bitter," June 7, 1928, p. 3.

"Delegates Bought, Norris Declares," June 8, 1928, p. 3.

"Texas Delegates Are Confederate Sons," June 10, 1928, p. 7.

"Committee Votes to Seat 43 Delegates for Hoover from Texas, Florida and Louisiana," June 13, 1928, p. 2.

"Part of Texas Delegation Seated After Fight," June 14, 1928, p. 3.

"Organization Upset by National Committee Vote to Unseat Delegation to Republican National Convention," June 5, 1928, p. 1.

"National Convention to Pass on Dispute Over Seating of Certain Delegates," May 31, 1928, p. 3.

"Mississippi Negro Leaders Rest Aimed from Holding Company and State Elections to Name Delegates to National Convention," March 12, 1928, p. 2.

"Seating of Delegates," May 28, 1928, p. 25.

"Seats Contested," June 4, 1928, p. 4.

"Radio Version of Fight of Texas Delegates," June 14, 1928, p. 9.

1956

W. H. Lawrence, "Four Leaders Face Ouster by G.O.P," April 19, 1956, p. 15.

"Racial Group Split G.O.P. in Mississippi, " May 6, 1956, p. 72.

"Battle at Convention Seen Over Mississippi and South Carolina Members, " April 19, 1956, p. 15.

"Comment on Racial Issues as Basic to Mississippi Contest, " May 6, 1956, p. 72.

"Tennessee G.O.P. Hits High Court, " July 1, 1956, p. 46.

"Southern Republicans, " November 20, 1956, p. 30.

APPENDIX II

POLITICAL SCIENCE EDUCATION IN THE BLACK COLLEGE

by Hanes Walton, Jr. and Brenda D. Mobley

Of what relevance are politics, political socialization and political education to the improvement of Black self-concepts and self-images? The relevance of politics and political education "to objective Black effectiveness in society and hence to the cultivation of higher self-esteem is perhaps best understood if one can grasp the relationship of the individual citizen to Democracy."[1]

Democracy is based on the concept of an alert and intelligent citizenry. The people in a democracy must grasp, comprehend, and appreciate the character of their society, its goals and purposes, its limitations, its methods of operation, and the boundaries of reasonable choice in their nation and the world of which they are a part.[2] Although every form of political order requires citizens with a certain level of knowledge and particular skills, a democratic nation, if it is to exist, must have citizens who understand their political system and its setup. This is necessarily so because people of a democracy play an active role in public affairs and, at times, eventually prescribe national policy. Thus, they must be acquainted with ways and means of ordering and using knowledge concerning political matters.

A progressive democratic society ultimately depends upon an alert citizenry, which is ready, willing and able to

146

participate in public affairs. In fact, the degree to which a citizen can participate in his government in a democratic society is indicative of that society's perceptions of his total worth as an individual. As Professor Seasholes aptly states, "political effectiveness reinforces an individual's general sense of personal adequacy in the society at large" because negative feelings about the political system and general political ineffectiveness "too often induce negative feelings about the self."[3]

Hence, if a democratic society blocks or hampers the participation of any group in that society, low involvement and low effectiveness are indeed the expected results. Beyond these factors are the emergence of attitudes such as political cynicism, political alienation and frustrations that are the natural outgrowth of non-participation. Concomitant with the negative attitudes are negative self-images or concepts; the blocked group has cause to believe that their own government believes them to be worthless or useless in the political structure of society and its policies. All of the groups (Blacks, women, youth) which have been excluded from participation in America's political arena have protested in many ways, but most consistently on the basis of the denial of their worth as persons and citizens.

It is not necessary to mention how Blacks have been denied participation in the American political arena, in varying degrees of intensity at one time or another in this country's political history. The resultant low political efficiency and the resulting poor self-image have been recounted many times. Numerous political scientists have alluded to the tremendous degree of political apathy within the black community and several politicians have blamed it for their political defeats.

To correct the problem, several individuals have looked to the public education system "to demonstrate more clearly the relevance of politics as a means" for Blacks to achieve their ends and improve their self-image at the same time.[4]

Since the southern public school system, as well as the northern system, tended "to inculcate [Blacks] with the prevailing norm of political behavior for that race, namely non-involvement," especially before the late sixties, this study shifts its focus to the nature of political education in Black colleges.

A survey of Black colleges in 1968 revealed that from the outset these schools had a profound understanding of the value of political education and sought to provide it in their curriculum.[5] However, the teaching of the courses focused primarily upon description, explanation and theory rather than upon involvement, practice, and manipulation of the system for the achievement of goals. In short, political science education at Black colleges became something of an ivory tower which offered little of practical value.

At first in most Black colleges, political science education didn't exist; in others it was represented only as a single general education course; yet others provided it as a part of a general social science course.[6] In larger Black colleges, Political Science was a junior department and didn't achieve independent status until the late fifties and early sixties. Where it did emerge as a separate discipline, it did so because of outside prodding, because Political Science was a part of the curriculum of white schools; although lack of staff, money, and facilities also operated to limit the emergence of political science as a separate discipline before the late fifties.

In 1968, 40% of the 81 Black colleges in this survey offered a degree program in Political Science and 17% had a minor concentration. On the other hand, 43% had no program concentration at all.

Among the courses[7] offered at Black schools, American Government was offered by 88% of all the Black institutions analyzed. While all of the colleges with either a major or a minor offer this course, only 77% of those with no concentration included it in their curricula. Following American Government was International Relations, which was part of the curriculum of 72% of all the schools studied; being offered at 97% of the colleges with a major, 93% with a minor, and 38% of those with no concentration.

Political Theory--at one time "considered one of the 'must' courses in the political science curriculum"--is included in the offering of 55% of the Black colleges. Eighty-eight (88%) per cent of those colleges offering a major have it, while 78% of those with a minor and 18% of those with no concentration have it.

The course in Comparative Government, described as a "universal requirement" in the previous study, has apparently lost some of its status. Only 91% with a major concentration, 78% of those with a minor concentration, and 38% of those with no concentration continue to offer it.

Courses in American Government and Politics are required at 91% of those colleges with a major, 78% of those with a minor, and 74% without a concentration. The same situation, however, does not prevail with courses in Public Administration, which are not offered by 70% of the colleges: 34% of those with a major, 86% of those colleges with a minor, and 94% of those with no concentration do not provide them.

Courses in public or constitutional law (which one would expect to find in all curricula because of their focus upon the problem of civil liberties) are infrequently offered in the Black colleges. Of the entire group of institutions investigated, 62% failed to see the significance and necessity of such courses. Although 62% of the schools with a major concentration included them, 72% of those offering a minor concentration and 88% of the other schools did not.

Courses in research and methodology, as well as seminar courses which might combine the two with independent study and reading, are offered by 62% of the Black colleges with a major, 21% with a minor, 9% with no concentration, and only 34% of the total sample.

Last but not least, courses on Black Politics are almost non-existent. In fact, the survey revealed that only three Black colleges in 1968 (Fisk, Howard, and Lincoln University) offered such a course.

With the great number of Black politicians emerging after the 1965 Voting Rights Act and the tremendous sacrifice of money, time and human life that Blacks had made in an effort to get to the political arena, it would seem that such courses would have been offered. But, since white colleges excluded courses on Black Politics and since Blacks have traditionally been almost totally excluded from the political arena, Black educational institutions continued to exclude the Black man, even intellectually, from the political arena. Black political education left the Black man's trials and tribulations in politics out of the curriculum as a special course. The black colleges failed signally to educate the Black man to the possibilities of politics as a means to an end, or as a means to achieving his goal.

Seeing this omission and the need for a reversal in

course offerings and a positive political socialization of Blacks in their own colleges, Professor Jewel Prestage, Chairman of the Department of Political Science at Southern University, with some foundation support began a study of Black colleges' Political Science curricula, with hopes of rearranging them to include courses on Black Politics.[8] At this writing, her efforts are still in progress and hopefully they will succeed.

Summarizing then, while the Black colleges may have succeeded in offering their students a reasonable insight into the American political system, they have failed to emphasize the efforts and activities of their own group. Black Politics courses, as the study revealed, were scarcely taught, and the possibility of the political approach as a means to an end went unexplored by Black colleges. Moreover, Black political education at Black colleges did little to improve the negative self-images and concepts that emerged from Black noninvolvement in politics. In fact, Black colleges helped to perpetuate the prevailing attitudes of society around them-- i.e., politics was white folk business--by not demonstrating to their students the tremendous efforts Blacks had made and were making to make politics useful to the Black community.

Notes

1. Bradbury Seasholes, "Political Socialization of Negroes: Image Development of Self and Polity, " in W. C. Kvaraceus, et al. (eds.), Negro Self-Concepts (New York: McGraw-Hill, 1965), p. 70-71.

2. R. E. Cleary & D. H. Riddle, "Political Science in the Social Studies, " in R. E. Cleary & D. H. Riddle (eds.), Political Science in the Social Studies, Vol. 36 (Washington, D.C.: National Council for Social Studies, 1966), p. 1.

3. Seasholes, op. cit., p. 52 and 72.

4. Ibid., p. 88.

5. For an earlier survey of political education in Black colleges see T. Barker, "Political Science in Institutions of Higher Learning for Negroes: Some Observations on Departmental Organization and Curriculum," Quarterly Review of Higher Education Among Negroes (July, 1959), p. 139. See also Merze Tate, "The Teaching of International Relations in Negro Colleges," Quarterly Review of Higher Education Among Negroes (July, 1947), pp. 149-154.

6. Irving A. Derbigny, General Education in the Negro College (Stanford: Stanford University Press, 1947), pp. 160-194.

7. The course categories which follow are based upon the grouping used in Albert Somit and Joseph Tananhaus, American Political Science: A Profile of a Discipline (New York: Atherton Press, 1964), pp. 52, 54, 56. See also Barker, op. cit., p. 139-149.

8. See Jewel Prestage, "Report of the Conference on Political Science Curriculum at Predominantly Black Institutions," P. S. (Summer, 1969), pp. 322-336. See also Lenneal Henderson, Jr., "Engineers of Black Liberation," The Black Politician (April, 1970), pp. 12-16.

Author Index

154

159

160